THE

DIARY

OF

DR. THOMAS CARTWRIGHT,

BISHOP OF CHESTER;

COMMENCING AT THE TIME OF HIS ELEVATION TO THAT SEE,

AUGUST M.DC.LXXXVI.;

AND TERMINATING WITH THE VISITATION OF ST. MARY MAGDALENE

COLLEGE, OXFORD, OCTOBER M.DC.LXXXVII.

———————

NOW FIRST PRINTED FROM THE ORIGINAL MS.

IN THE POSSESSION OF

THE REV. JOSEPH HUNTER, F.S.A.

WIPF & STOCK · Eugene, Oregon

Wipf and Stock Publishers
199 W 8th Ave, Suite 3
Eugene, OR 97401

Diary of Dr. Thomas Cartwright, Bishop of Chester
Commencing at the Time of His Elevation to that See,
August M.DC.LXXXVI
By Cartwright, Thomas
Softcover ISBN-13: 978-1-7252-9145-4
Hardcover ISBN-13: 978-1-7252-9144-7
eBook ISBN-13: 978-1-7252-9146-1
Publication date 11/3/2020
Previously published by Camden Society, 1843

This edition is a scanned facsimile of
the original edition published in 1843.

PREFACE.

BISHOP CARTWRIGHT was educated at Oxford, and is
accordingly noticed by Wood, whose summary of the
principal events of his life contains nearly all the information concerning him which the Reader will require as
preparatory to the perusal of the following Diary.

" THOMAS CARTWRIGHT, son of Thomas Cartwright,
sometimes schoolmaster of Brentwood in Essex, was born
in the antient borough of Northampton, on the 1st Sept.
1634, educated in the school there, and being puritani-
cally educated under Presbyterian parents, was sent to
Magdalene Hall, where spending two terms in the study
of logic, was forcibly put into Queen's College by the
visitors appointed by parliament, anno 1649, and at that
time he was put under the tuition of Mr. Thomas Tully.
Afterwards he was made Tabarder and Chaplain of the
College for a time; but before he was elected Fellow,
he left the house (having before been ordained priest by
Dr. Robert Skinner, Bishop of Oxon), and became vicar
of Walthamstow in Essex, and a very forward and confi-

dent preacher for the cause then in being. In 1659 I find him chaplain to John Robinson, Esq. Alderman, and then Sheriff of London, and a preacher at St. Mary Magdalene, in Milk Street; but whether he did then enjoy the vicarage of Barking in Essex, which he did after his Majesty's restoration, I cannot tell. After the King's return he showed himself very forward to express his loyalty, and was made domestic chaplain to Henry Duke of Gloucester, procured himself to be actually created Doctor of Divinity, though not of full standing for it; was made Prebendary of Twyford in the cathedral church of St. Paul, minister of St. Thomas Apostle in London, prebendary of Shalford in the church of Wells, and chaplain in ordinary to his Majesty. In Nov. 1672, he was installed Prebend of Durham, struck in on the death of Dr. Tully his quondam tutor, and was made Dean of Ripon, in the latter end of 1675. Afterwards putting in with great boldness before his seniors for a bishoprick, particularly that of St. David, but put aside by Dr. L. Womack, was at length made Bishop of Chester on the death of the most learned and religious Dr. John Pearson, to which see being consecrated with Dr. Lloyd to St. David, and Dr. Parker to Oxon, at Lambeth, on 17th Oct. 1686, had liberty then allowed to him to keep the vicarage of Barking, and the rectory of Wigan in Lancashire, which he before had obtained in commendam with

his bishoprick. In the next year, he being then in favour
with King James the Second, and ready upon all occasions to run with his humour, purposely to obtain a
translation to a better bishoprick, he was by him not only
added to the number of Ecclesiastical Commissioners, but
also appointed one of the three Delegates or Commissioners (Sir Robert Wright, Chief Justice of the King's
Bench, and Sir Thomas Jenner, one of the Barons of the
Exchequer, being the other two,) to go to Oxon to
examine and determine the affairs relating to Magdalene
College, and what they did there in ejecting the President
and Fellows thereof, a book, entitled, " An Impartial
Relation of the illegal proceedings against St. Mary
Magdalene College, in Oxon," &c. Lond. 1689, 4to. sec.
edit. collected by a Fellow of that College, will at large
tell you. At that time this Bishop making it his sole
endeavour to be gracious with the then great and lead-
ing men, and to show himself in all public assemblies,
particularly in those wherein the Roman Catholic Bishops
were consecrated, he gained the ill-will so much of the
sons of the Church of England, that when the Prince of
Aurange made his expedition into England, he out of fear
of suffering for what he had acted, and of the insults of
the rabble (then committing great disorders in London
and most parts of the nation), did withdraw himself in
private, skulk, and in a disguise fled into France; where

repairing to his royal master King James the Second, then lately come thither to avoid imminent danger in England, had by him, on the news of Dr. Ward's death, the bishoprick of Salisbury conferred on him; and while he abode at St. Germain's, he did usually read the Liturgy of the Church of England in his lodgings to such Protestants that came thither to him. Afterwards he went with his said master towards Ireland, landed there on Tuesday 12th March, 1688, and on Sunday following being at Cork, he received the Sacrament from the hands of the Bishop of that place. On Palm Sunday, March 24th, he went to Dublin with the King, and on Easter day and the Octaves of Easter 1689, he again received the Sacrament at Christ Church there, from the Bishop of Meath, to which church Bishop Cartwright went daily to prayers. Afterwards being overtaken with the country disease called the flux or dysentery, he finished his course there on Monday morning, April 15, 1689." Wood then gives a list of his printed Sermons. We have afterwards an account of some circumstances of his latest moments, (from which the inference is drawn that he showed an aversion to Popery,) and also of the honours paid him at his funeral. He was buried in Christ Church, Dublin.[a]

a Ath. Oxon. fol. 1692, vol. ii. col. 629—631.

Burnet speaks of him thus :

"The other two Bishopricks were less considerable :
so they resolved to fill them with the two worst men that
could be found out. Cartwright was promoted to Chester. He was a man of good capacity, and had made
some progress in learning. He was ambitious and servile,
cruel and boisterous ; and, by the great liberties he
allowed himself, he fell under much scandal of the worst
sort. He set himself long to raise the King's authority
above law ; which he said was only a method of government to which Kings might submit as they pleased : but
their authority was from God, absolute and superior to
law, which they might exert as oft as they found it necessary for the ends of government. So he was looked on
as a man that would more effectually advance the designs
of Popery, than if he should turn over to it. And,
indeed, bad as he was, he never made that step even in
the most desperate state of his affairs." [a]

Richardson's description of this Prelate is even more
severe :

"Thomas Cartwright, a Jacobo, jam tum in ecclesiâ res
novas moliente, ad hanc Diocesin evocatus est ; eo ipso
dignus habitus qui in Ecclesiâ Anglicanâ ad sedem Epis-
copalem promoveretur, quòd ad ipsius ornamentum aut

---

[a] Hist. of his Own Times, Oxford, 8vo. 1823, vol. iii. p. 136.

B

tutelam adeo nihil afferret, ut ejus proditor et transfuga
in pontificiorum castra transire semper esset paratus.
Adeoque postea rerum jam potito Gulielmo, Jacobum
comitatus in Hiberniam Ecclesiæ Romanæ fidem publicè
profitebatur, ibique vitam terminavit decimo quinto Aprilis
1689."[a]

Whether any thing that is peculiarly harsh in what
is said of Bishop Cartwright is to be attributed to
party prejudice, or that all is sufficiently borne out by
facts, it does not appear that any person has come
forward to vindicate his memory, but that this estimate
of him has passed into the general current of history
and human opinion.

One recent writer only may be referred to.

Sir James Mackintosh ascribes his elevation to the
episcopal dignity to the courtly doctrines inculcated by
him in Sermons which he afterwards printed and circu-
lated, and speaks also of the grosser charges contained in
the passage quoted from Burnet.[b]

Whether any thing which is recorded in this Diary by
the Bishop's own hand will, when compared with other
historical facts, deepen any of the darker shades of his
character, or set his conduct in a fairer light, may be
left to be determined by the reader, and by those who

[a] Godwin, de Præsulibus Angliæ, fol. 1743, p. 779.
[b] History of the Revolution in England in 1688, p. 70.

may hereafter use the amount of secret history contained in this Diary in any critical review of the period to which it belongs. It is published with no purpose of pressing upon the memory of one who, whatever may have been his faults, is gone to his account, or, on the other hand, of clearing away any of the clouds which rest upon his memory. This open promulgation of it is made simply with the view of placing in the hands of persons who may be engaged in the study of the period of history (undoubtedly a critical and most memorable period) to which it relates, what it is not too much to designate as an *historical document* of a curious character, on which, as far as it goes, the most perfect reliance may be placed ; a document which admits us to some acquaintance, not before possessed, with the secret transactions of the time, and particularly with those which had reference to the then very hazardous state of the Reformed Church of England.

That more may not however be expected from this Diary than it will be found to contain, it is proper to add, that it is merely a recital of occurrences, many of them of no importance, written down with a hasty and careless pen, day by day, useful memoranda to which afterwards to refer, and seldom with any thing of motive or opinion: the private record of his private life, sprinkled however with many passages which concern the public; and nothing can be plainer than that it was written with not the most distant expectation that it would ever be regarded as part of the materials for our national history.

In the use of a private record of this nature, when it has passed from the hands of those who are the legitimate possessors, and also the natural guardians of a dead man's reputation, there is undoubtedly a reserve to be used; and even the lapse of more than a century may not be sufficient to justify the publication of every thing which a man has left in writing, in the confidence that it would fall under no observation but that of those who would have a natural and tender regard for his memory. But this reserve must not be carried too far: and it may require to be set aside, out of regard to the higher interest of preserving the stream of history pure, and especially when such a document exhibits fully and clearly what a prominent actor in any historical period thought and did. Without such materials as these, we should have no authentic history of events which have influenced our social and political condition : and it is not perhaps too much to say, that we shall have a juster apprehension of the course of events which led up to the Revolution of 1688, and understand more fully the imminent hazard in which the Reformed Church of England was placed, now that this Diary is added to the original materials for the history of those times. When this is the case, there is surely sufficient to justify the sacrifice of some degree of delicate reserve, and to save the Society harmless, who placed this private Diary in the list of its Manuscripts deserving publication. At the worst, the publication of an authentic record of his proceedings, at the distance of a hundred and fifty years from the time of his death, is but the price which is paid by one who allowed himself to interfere to a great extent with the religion and liberties of his country, and who trod, though but for a short time, the paths of a high ambition in the full sunshine of the favour of his royal master.

Of private family affairs, or personal habits, there is little, if any thing, to which the reserve spoken of can apply. If any thing ought to be left out of this publication, from regard to that reserve, it is matter peculiarly relating to the Bishop's public life, and therefore what it is peculiarly necessary to make public. We find throughout, this Protestant Bishop in constant communication with the Roman Catholics of the time, both those whom he found in his own diocese, and those who were more especially the agents for the Court of Rome, in the design of re-uniting England to the Church of which Rome was the head, and communicating with them apparently on matters of the greatest importance to the wellbeing of the church.

At the same time, it may not be unseasonable to present before the reader the words of one of the most

sensible and kind-hearted of our old authors, whose name
it will be unnecessary to mention when the lines are read,
which are so full of his peculiar genius and character:
" Now, an exact Diary is a window into his heart that
maketh it, and therefore pity it is that any eyes should
look therein, but either the friends of the party, or such
ingenious foes as will not (especially in things doubtful)
make conjectural comments to his disgrace." [a]

It has not been discovered who are the present repre-
sentatives of the Bishop, who, though born in Northamptonshire, is not supposed to belong to the existing family of
Cartwright of Aynho. It will be seen that the Bishop had
several sons, and many relatives are named by him, most
of whom appear to have resided in that county. In the
manuscript is the book plate of " George Watkin, B.D.
of Lincoln College, Oxford ;" but the history of the manuscript has not been traced. Twelve or fourteen years
ago it was in the hands of a bookseller at Northampton, of
whom it was purchased by the gentleman from whom it
passed to the present possessor.

In form it is a small octavo, bound in black leather, and
is written throughout. The hand-writing is loose and
rambling, and there is the same inattention to uniformity
in orthography, especially of proper names, which prevails

---

[a] Church History of Britain, XVIIth Cent. p. 218.

through most of the manuscript of England down to a recent period. It also abounds in contracted forms, and words but half written, and in some places there are passages which are written in characters. The system of short-hand which the Bishop used bespeaks his Puritan origin. It is that of Rich, which appears to have been constructed for the peculiar purpose of taking down the Sermons of Puritan Divines, and which long continued to be in general use among the descendants of the Puritans, and is so even to the present day.

In this publication no regard is paid to the contractions or the mere carelessnesses of orthography in the original manuscript: but as the passages written in characters are for the most part passages of more curiosity than the rest, and it may be presumed that recourse was had to that mode of writing for secrecy as well as for expedition, it has been thought proper to distinguish such passages by placing them within crotchets.

In a very few instances, the transcriber has met with difficulties such as are sometimes found in deciphering epistles of our friends at the present day. If there should therefore be here and there a slight error, it is hoped that it may be pardoned. If the passage was in any respect material, a doubtful word has been dotted out. With this exception, the whole Diary is given without any curtailment, not omitting even entries which, separately considered,

are wholly unimportant. Certain official documents relating
to the Bishop's elevation to the See of Chester, which the
book contains, it has been thought unnecessary to publish.

It was the original intention that this Diary should be
printed as an historical document, without any species of
annotation, in the same manner as the Diary of Henry Earl
of Clarendon, of nearly the same period, was published.
The public taste however, it is said, requires an apparatus
of notes to all publications of this nature, and, in defer-
ence to that taste, a few are added explanatory of some
of the circumstances and events noticed in the Diary, or
intended to identify persons named, and thus to save the
trouble of a reference. All idea of doing more was set
aside as unsuitable to a publication of this nature. The
attempt has not even been made to identify every person
whom the writer names, those only of some distinction
being noticed. Such an effort would have been attended
with an expense of time and labour wholly dispropor-
tionate to the occasion ; and would, at last, in many cases,
have proved ineffectual; and this, even though I have
been favoured with the assistance of one who is so inti-
mately acquainted with all the minuter parts of the history
of the period, as is the noble Lord who honours the Camden Society by taking a part in the direction of its affairs.

Lord Braybrooke, it may be added, has a peculiar interest in one principal event to which much in this Diary re-

lates ; no one having more distinguished himself in the memorable stand which the Fellows of Magdalene College made against the attempt upon their just rights and privileges, than did their Vice-President, Dr. Charles Aldworth, who was brother of Richard Aldworth, Esq. his Lordship's paternal ancestor. Many original letters and papers connected with the Visitation of the College, and copies of other documents relating to it, collected by Dr. Aldworth, are now in his Lordship's possession, and have supplied matter for the notes. To him also the Society is indebted for very much of any other useful information which the notes may be found to contain.

J. H.

THE DIARY

OF

DR. THOMAS CARTWRIGHT, &c.

August 1686.

11. King James the Second, my most gracious master, called me aside in his bedchamber at Windsor this morning, and promised me the Bishoprick of Chester, and he published the same in the Cabinet Council on Sunday the 22d of August; and declared Dr. Samuel Parker at the same time to be Bishop of Oxon, and we kissed the King's, Queen's, and Princess Anne of Denmark's hands that night at Windsor.

24. I din'd at Lambeth. Letters sent to the Earl of Peterborough [a] and the Dean of Durham, [b] Dr. Grey, Mr. Mickelton, Sir Medcalfe Robinson,[c] the Bishops of Lincoln and Lichfield.[d]

26. Letters to the Marquess of Winchester,[e] Dr. Watkinson.[f]

---

[a] Henry Mordaunt, the second Earl, a great friend of the new Bishop, who, on one occasion, calls him his patron. They were in very frequent communication. He was at this time, like the Bishop, advanced in life, having distinguished himself in the Civil Wars more than forty years before. He was a professed Roman Catholic, and in great esteem with King James, who made him Groom of the Stole on his accession.

[b] Dr. Dennis Granvile, who refusing in 1690 to take the oaths to the new Government, was deprived of his deanery.

[c] Of Newby, near Ripon, where Cartwright had been Dean. He was created a Baronet on the Restoration, and served in three parliaments for York.

[d] Dr. Thomas Barlow and Dr. James Wood.

[e] Charles Paulet, the sixth Marquess, living at this period at his castle of Bolton, taking no part in public affairs; but when the Prince of Orange had landed, exerting himself to give success to his designs; for which he was rewarded by the Dukedom of Bolton.

[f] Henry Watkinson, LL.D., Chancellor of the Church of York.

September.

2.   Letters to P. Whalley,[a] Mr. Archer.

9.   Letters to Marquess of Winchester, brother Stow, Mr. Harvey, Mr. Holmes.

13.   Letters to Dr. Watkinson, Dean of York,[b] Dean of Chester,[c] Governor of Chester,[d] Mr. Archer, Marquess of Winchester, Mr. Mickelton :—

14.   I married Dr. Wainwright[e] and Rebecca Jackson, at Stepney church.

23.   —— Mr. Greswold, Mr. Holmes, and Dr. Watkinson.

26.   I preached for Sir William Holcroft at Layton.

29.   The King signed a warrant for my holding of Barking and Wigan in commendam, at Windsor, after which I returned that night to London and wrote letters to Brother Stow, P. Whalley, Mr. Mickelton.

30.   I dined at Lambeth, and delivered my warrant for the commendam, Sir Thomas Exton and Dr. Raines being there.[f] The Lord Chancellor, refusing to pass the Royal Assent to me, went out of town.[g]

[a] Rector of Cogenhoe in Northamptonshire from 1656 to the time of his decease in April 1701.   The Bishop speaks of him afterwards as a relation.

[b] Dr. Tobias Wickham, who was succeeded by the learned Gale.

[c] Dr. James Ardern, or Arden.   His name will frequently occur as " Mr. Dean." According to Wood (Ath. Ox. Bliss' edit. Fasti an. 1673), his views were nearly co-incident with those of Cartwright, and it was understood that he would succeed Cartwright in the Bishoprick of Chester, in the event of Cartwright's elevation to any other dignity.   Yet it appears that on October 6, 1687, the Bishop suspended him from his office.   In his will, which is printed by Ormerod (Cheshire, vol. ii. p. 40), he declares that he dies " in the communion of the Catholic Church, and more immediately of that part of it in England."

[d] Probably Sir Geoffery Shakerley, who died in 1696, aged 78, and was Governor of Chester at the time of his death.

[e] Probably Thomas Wainwright, LL.D. Chancellor of the Church of Chester, 1682.

[f] Sancroft was then the Archbishop ; Sir Thomas Exton was his Vicar-General ; Dr. Raines, a civilian, Judge of the Prerogative Court, afterwards Judge of the High Court of Admiralty, and knighted.

[g] Neither the Archbishop nor the Chancellor (Jeffries) approved of the elevation of Cartwright to the episcopal dignity, and they had endeavoured to place the Chan-

October.

1. The King and Queen returned safe to Whitehall.[a]

3. I preached at St. Augustine's in London, and received the sacrament there, and was kindly entertained at Mrs. Rigby's, Mr. J. Ashton's father-in-law, my son, and Mr. Callis, with me.

4. I entertained the Bishops of Oxon and St. David's,[b] Mr. Ashton, Mr. Brookes, my son, Mr. Callis, &c. at the Blue Posts in the Haymarket.

5. I was kindly entertained at dinner with my son at the Bishop of Durham's.[c]

6. I was kindly entertained by Mr. Coles at the Blue Anchor; after which my son and I went and made a visit to the Bishop of Ely[d] at Ely house.

7. I was at the King's levee, dined with the chaplains, and sent letters to Dr. Watkinson, brother Stow. I went with Mr. Taylor and delivered the king's preachers' petition for their two years' salary to my Lord Treasurer, which he kindly received, and promised payment.[e] This night my Lord Chancellor returned to his house

cellor's brother in the seat in which Cartwright was placed by the King. (Mackintosh, p. 71.) There was no good understanding between Jeffries and Cartwright; and on one occasion, two years after the time of which we are speaking, Cartwright received a rebuke from the King for saying in his cups that Jeffries and Sunderland would deceive him. (Ib. p. 143.)

[a] From a short progress which they had made in the West.

[b] Dr. Samuel Parker and Dr. John Lloyd. The latter held the Bishoprick of St. David's only a few months.

[c] Dr. Nathaniel Crew, who in 1691 succeeded to the inheritance of the family barony. He was Clerk of the Closet, and a principal member of the ecclesiastical commission which King James had appointed. His views were not very strongly opposed to those of the Bishop of Chester, though personally there existed no very cordial esteem between them, at least not on the part of the Bishop of Durham. We shall see that the two Bishops were often together.

[d] Dr. Francis Turner. He was, like Sancroft, a Non-juror after the Revolution, and deprived.

[e] This was done in his new character of Bishop of Chester; the persons intended by "the King's preachers" being the itinerating preachers of Lancashire, a part of his diocese, successors to a body of four ministers established in the reign of Elizabeth. Mr. Taylor, who accompanied the Bishop, was one of the preachers: Dr. Zachary

in Queen Street and sealed the royal assent, and the commendam to me the next morning.

8. I was at the King's levee, dined with Sir John Peake, Lord Mayor elect, and Sir John More.[a]

9. I waited on the Lord Chancellor with the Bishop of St. David's, dined with the chaplains, and lodged at my cousin Margaret's. Letters to cousins Whalley, Dr. Hooke,[b] Mr. Milner,[c] Dr. Pemberton.

10. I preached at Stepney, dined with Mr. Shephard, and lodged the night before at my cousin Margaret's, and visited Captain Haddock.

11. My Lord Chancellor deferred the sealing of my commendam till this day, with whom the Bishop of St. David's and I dined.

12. I was confirmed, with the Bishops of St. David's and Oxford,[d] in Bow Church; and dined at Doctors' Commons, where my guests were Sir John Lowther,[e] Sir Roger L'Estrange,[f] Sir Edmund Wiseman,[g] my son John, and Mr. Rigby.

Taylor, author of the tract in which a rational account is given of the disease and cure of Dugdale, the supposed dæmoniac of Surey in Lancashire.

[a] Sir John More had been Lord Mayor the year but one before.

[b] Dr. Richard Hooke, the Vicar of Halifax, who, during the reign of Charles the Second, had been a very active opposer of the non-conformity which prevailed to a great extent in his large parish.

[c] The Vicar of Leeds of that name; one of those men of high conscientiousness who resigned their preferment rather than comply with the requisition to take the oaths to King William.

[d] It is remarkable that of the three Bishops confirmed this day, there are two of them upon whom posterity has not looked without some reserve in its respect, Cartwright of Chester and Parker of Oxford: but the higher and purer minds probably saw through the King's intentions, and were content to remain for the present in more private stations. Of the venerable men who retired from their stations in the church on the new settlement at the Revolution, not one of the Bishops, nor I think any of the other dignitaries, and but few of the ordinary clergy, had owed their preferment to King James.

[e] Knight of the shire for Cumberland.

[f] The famous political writer of that name.

[g] A younger son of Sir William Wiseman, of Canfield-hall in Essex, by a sister of the Lord Capel who was put to death in the time of the Commonwealth.

13. I was at the King's levee at Whitehall. I gave £100 this day towards the repairs of St. Paul's church, for which I have the Receiver-general's acquittance. Mr. Lawrence Spencer and I entertained Sir Roger L'Estrange and my *fidus Achates* at night.

14. This being the King's birth day, I attended him at his levee, and was very graciously received by him. Dined with the Bishop of Durham. Sent letters to [the] Dean of Chester; cousin Whalley; and heard the songs to the King in the evening.

15. I was with the King in the morning with the Bishop of St. David's; dined with my Lord Preston; a discoursed with the King as he went to council; entertained Mr. Ware, Mr. Tucker, Dr. Th . . . . , and Mr. Davis, at night.

16. I gave Mr. Zachary Taylor, the King's preacher, two receipts for £400 due to him and his brethren at Michaelmas last past. Went over with the Bishop of St. David's to dine at Lambeth. I sealed a letter of attorney to Mr. John Allen, to receive my Michaelmas pension from the King's receiver at Chester. I gave Hugh King, an old footman of the Duke of Glocester's, 5s. Wrote to [the] Marquess of Winchester and Mr. Robert Mann, of Lincoln, and supped with Dr. Busby at Westminster.

17. I was with the Bishop of Oxford at the King's levee; where he having received notice of the King's pleasure by my Lord Sunderland that I should be consecrated before him (though confirmed after him by the contrivance of my Lord Chancellor, at which the King expressed his high displeasure), urged my Lord Sunderland to signify to the King that it would be a thing against all precedents and much to his dissatisfaction, whereupon his lordship (having consulted the King in his closet) signified to me that the King would take it kindly of me if I would waive my pretensions to seniority, which he acknowledged to be just, and that I

---

a Originally Sir Richard Graham, Bart. of Netherby, in Cumberland; created Baron Graham of Esk and Viscount Preston, Scotish honours, in 1681. He adhered to the fortunes of the house of Stuart, and was forfeited in 1690.

should suddenly receive such a mark of his royal favour as would more than compensate my present claim. After this we went in the Archbishop's barge from the Privy Stairs to Lambeth, with the Bishops of Durham, Norwich,[a] and Ely, and there met the Bishop of Rochester,[b] who joined with the Archbishop in our consecration. Mem. The Archbishop fell flat on his face as he passed with the Holy Bread from the south to the north side of the altar, his head to the place where he knelt; but being raised up by his two chaplains, Dr. Morice and Dr. Batley, he proceeded well to the end of the service.[c] Mr. Lowth preached the consecration sermon. The Bishop of St. David's and I went that night to the King's Chapel at Whitehall to prayers, and after attended his Majesty, who was graciously pleased to send us word by his secretaries that we should be admitted to do our homage the next day. Sir John Lowther, Sir William Meredith,[d] Sir Edmund Wiseman, Mr. Poultney, Mr. Thame, and Mr. Callis, visited me that night. We gave guineas a piece for our offering.

18. St. Luke's day. This morning I went to the King's levee, did my homage with the Bishops of St. David's and Oxford, at eleven, dined with the Bishop of Oxford and his lady, and the Bishop of Rochester. Met Serjeant Killinghall at Mr. Cooke's.

19. I was at the King's levee, gave the drum and trumpeters

---

[a] Dr. William Lloyd, another of the non-juring Bishops, and deprived.

[b] Dr. Thomas Sprat. He acted in King James's commission, yet complied at the Revolution.

[c] Burnet gives rather a different version of this story :—"Some of the Bishops brought to the Archbishop articles against Cartwright and Parker, and he promised Bishop Lloyd not to consecrate them till he had examined the truth of those articles; yet when he saw what danger he might incur if he were sued in a præmunire, he consented to consecrate them. An accident happened in the action that struck him much. When he was going to give the chalice in the sacrament, he stumbled on one of the steps of the altar, and dashed out all the consecrated wine that was in it; which was much taken notice of, and gave himself the more trouble, since he was frightened to such a consecration by so mean a fear."—Own Times, 8vo. 1823, vol. iii. p. 138.

[d] Of Henbury in Cheshire, the second Baronet.

10*s*.; Mrs. Hambden and another poor widow money. Visited the Bishop of Lincoln; dined with my Lord Halifax[a] and Sir John Lowther. Visited Bishop Labourne,[b] where I met father Ellis;[c] supped at Mr. Thompson's, with Mr. Cooke, Mr. Wooddard, and Dr. Starkey, chaplain to the Earl of Dover, &c.

20. I visited Sir Thomas Fanshaw and his lady, and my Lord Fanshaw, at Mr. Charles Fanshaw's lodgings. I dined with Serjeant Killingworth; supped with Judge Wright, Mr. Hobbs, and Mr. Starkey,

21. I dined with the Earl of Dover,[d] with the Lord Colchester,[e] Lord Chief Justice Benningfield,[f] &c. Supped with Mr.

[a] George Savile, Marquis of Halifax. This was after he had been removed by King James from his post of President of the Council, in which he was succeeded by Lord Sunderland. He was a great promoter of the Revolution.

[b] A Roman Catholic Bishop, the only one then in England. He was auditor to Cardinal Howard, and invested with the episcopal character in this very year, when he immediately came to England, and on his arrival had lodgings assigned him at Whitehall, with a yearly pension of £1000 out of the privy purse.—Lingard, vol. xiv. p. 103. Cartwright, it will be seen, was in very frequent communication with him.

[c] This name will occur several times as we proceed. The person spoken of is Philip Ellis, who was son to a Protestant clergyman, and decoyed away, as it is said, from Westminster school by certain Jesuits, who brought him up a priest in the college of Saint Omer. He was in great favour at the Court of James the Second, and on Sunday, May 6, 1688, was consecrated a Bishop of the English Roman Catholic Church. On the change of affairs he left England, and was made Bishop of Segni in the Ecclesiastical States. His brother, who was the Protestant Bishop of Meath, was ancestor of the Clifden family.—See Account of the family of Ellis by the late Lord Dover prefixed to " The Ellis Correspondence," vol. i. p. xvii.

[d] There was no Earl of Dover at this period. The nobleman meant is doubtless Henry Jermyn, who was created Baron Jermyn of Dover at the beginning of the reign, and who was at this time a Lord of the Treasury, and at the same time Colonel of a troop of Guards.

[e] Richard Viscount Colchester, son and heir-apparent of Thomas Earl Rivers. He was an officer in Lord Dover's troop, and went over to the Prince of Orange from Salisbury.

[f] For Bedingfield: Sir Henry Bedingfield, Chief Justice of the Common Pleas. The peculiar orthography of the name in the text being uniform in the Diary, may serve to show how this surname was pronounced in those days.

John Cooke, Mr. Pollexfen, Mr. Jennings, and other lawyers of his neighbourhood.

22. I was at the King's levee, dined with Major Richardson, Serjeant Jefferson, Sir Edmund Wiseman, Mr. Snow, and the Major's brother, and Mr. Cooke, and supped with Mr. Cooke at Mr. Dreinard's.

23. I was at the King's levee. Dined with Dr. Hollingsworth,[a] Dr. Scot, and Mr. Hesketh, and kissed the Queen Dowager's hand that night at Somerset House.

24. I ordained John Pinchbeck, M.A. of Trinity College in Cambridge, Soc. priest, in Hen. 7th's chapel. Preached that morning in St. Anne's church in London, and dined with the Lord Preston, Sir Samuel Morland,[b] &c. Took my leave of the Lady Cony, the Bishops of Lincoln and St. David's.

25. I dined at Lambeth with the Bishop of Ely, took my leave of him and his Grace, with whom my successor the Dean of Ripon,[c] Col. Darcy, and Dr. Dove,[d] also dined. Visited my sister Barnard, Mr. Saint Ann,[e] Bishop of Durham, Sir William Meredith, and Mr. Cox.

26. I was at the King's levee, and kissed his hand, and had his leave to return into the North, with a gracious promise that he would never forget me nor my services, and that I should find his favour in all places and upon all occasions, and then recommended me to the Dean of Ripon for an Ex. . . . . I took my leave of my Lord of Durham, who received me with great expressions of kindness, dined with Mr. Duncomb and Mr. Backwell, supped with Mr. Vane and Sir Nath. Johnson, &c.[f]

---

[a] Probably Richard Hollingsworth, D.D. Vicar of West Ham, in Essex, and Rector of St. Botolph, Aldgate, and author of many sermons and religious tracts.

[b] The statesman and mechanician of the name.

[c] Dr. Christopher Wyvil.

[d] Henry Dove, D.D. Archdeacon of Richmond, 1678, who was minister of St. Bride's, and one of the Chaplains to Charles the Second and James the Second.

[e] Perhaps Saint Amand, written in haste and contractedly.

[f] Sir Nathaniel Johnson, made Captain-General of the Leeward Islands in August, 1686.—Pointer, p. 336.

27. I received several visits in the morning from Sir John Lowther, Sir Richard Allebone,[a] Sir William Stich, and others ; made up my accounts with Sir Edmund Wiseman; dined with Mr. De Puy and Mr. Ashton ; took my leave of my Lord Treconnel, who promised to make the palace at Chester his way to Ireland,[b] and said he hoped to live to see me Archbishop of Canterbury;[c] and kissed the Queen's hand in her bed-chamber, where she told me she nor the King would never forget my services to them before they were so, nor should I ever want a friend so long as she lived. I had my sons John, Gervas, and Richard, with me at supper, Sir William Meredith, Mr. Brookes, Dr. Yonger, &c.

28. St. Simon and St. Jude. I went out in the York coach from the Strand,[d] and came safe that night with Col. Douglas, Mr. Dean of Ripon, Mr. Cooke, Mrs. Vane, &c. to Stevenidge, from whence I wrote to Mr. Chancellor and Mr. Towres.

29. I came to Stamford, where I met my daughter Alicia, cousin P. Whalley, cousin Welsh and his wife, who supped and lodged there with me, and was visited by Mr. Mayor and his brethren, and four clergymen who invited me to preach there.

30. I preached at Stamford before the mayor, supped with the mayor, and afterwards was treated by Mr. Rogers with the clergy.

---

[a] The Roman Catholic Judge, who afterwards took so decided a part against the Seven Bishops.

[b] Whither he was going as Lord Lieutenant to succeed the Earl of Clarendon. We shall find that he visited the Bishop according to his promise.

[c] There are other passages like this, from which we may conclude that the Bishop was perpetually being flattered with hopes of higher preferment by the persons about the court, and by the King himself, with whom, however, he rose and fell.

[d] That it was the practice of those times for persons of rank to travel in the public stages is shewn by Mr. Markland in his curious paper on modes of travelling in England.—Archæologia, vol. xx. p. 443. The intermediate mode between travelling in the public stages and in private carriages with a gentleman's own horses, or what is called travelling post, or in chaises with horses furnished by the innkeepers on the road, does not seem to have been practised at this period in England, except in the case of expresses or hired messengers.

November.

1. I came safe to Newark.

2. To Doncaster.

3. To York, where I visited Mr. Dean, and after invited to supper with me Mr. Chancellor,[a] Mr. Holmes, Mr. Dean of Ripon, Mr. Stamford, Mr. William Jennings, Mr. Waite, Mr. Armitage, and Dr. Armitage, Mr. Weld, and was visited by Mr. Conyers, &c.

4. I went to prayers in the minster, and dined with Mr. Chancellor, and supped with Mr. Dean, where I received £3 rent of Mr. Bellingham of York, and granted a licence to George Bell to serve the cure of St. Cuthbert's in Barson, till farther order ; and drank with Mr. Hodgson and Mr. Risdell at night, and received a circular letter from the Dean and Chapter of York, from the High Commissioners at Whitehall.

5. I went from York to Ripon, accompanied by several gentlemen of Ripon, and was met by the way by the clergy of my diocese, and the mayor, and aldermen, and common council of the same, and supped at Ripon.

6. Mr. Dean of Ripon was installed, and I dined with him at Mr. Chambers' ; Sir Edmund Jennings,[b] Sir Marmaduke Wyvil,[c] and Sir Edward Blacket,[d] and six or seven clergymen of my diocese. Made up my accounts with the Dean and Chapter.

[a] Probably Christopher Stone, A.M. then Chancellor of the Church of York.

[b] Sir Edmund and Sir Jonathan Jennings were two brothers living at this time at Ripon. It was Sir Jonathan Jennings who, in the preceding reign, slew Mr. Aislabie, ancestor of the Studley family of that name, in a duel at York.

[c] Sir Marmaduke Wyvil of Constable Burton, the fifth Baronet, served in two parliaments for Richmond. His relations here mentioned were John, Prebendary of St. Paul's, and Vicar of Orset in Essex, son of Sir William the fourth Baronet ; Christopher, Dean of Ripon for twenty-four years ; and John, Receiver-General of the land-tax, who died in 1722, son of Sir Christopher Wyvil, the third Baronet.

[d] Sir Edward Blacket of Newby, 2d Baronet, served in several parliaments for Ripon or Northumberland.

7. I preached at Ripon, entertained Mr. Dean, Sir Marmaduke Wyvil, Mr. Fr. Wyvil and uxor, Mr. John Wyvil, Mr. Fr. Wyvil, Sir Richard Graham,[a] and his lady and daughter Elizabeth, and the Lady Purbeck,[b] Mr. Pemberton, Mr. Milner, &c. and the Vicars, at supper.

8. I was attended by Mr. Mayor of Ripon and his brethren, and visited Sir Jonathan Jennings at night.

9. I dined at Sir Edward Blacket's at Newby.

10. I dined with Sir Richard Graham at Norton, and lodged that night with Sir Medcalfe Robinson.

11. I came from Newby with Sir Medcalfe Robinson, in the Marquess's coach[c] to Bolton, where I met Mr. Mason and my Lord's chaplain, Mr. Hesleden and Mr. Bowes, and wrote that night advice to Mr. Cradock of my coming to Richmond on Saturday, in order to the preaching and confirmation there on Sunday.

12. I was received by the noble Marquess with all kindness imaginable at dinner from one at noon till one in the morning.[d] Sir

[a] Sir Richard Graham of Norton Conyers, a few miles distant from Ripon.

[b] Elizabeth, daughter of Sir William Slingsby, of Kippax Park in Yorkshire, a younger brother of Sir Henry Slingsby of Scriven, the second wife and widow of John Villiers the first Viscount Purbeck, who was probably living at this time with her relations in Yorkshire.

[c] The Marquess of Winchester.

[d] This sitting at table for twelve hours is to a certain extent a confirmation of the account which Granger gives from some contemporary memoirs, of the singular style in which this nobleman lived at his Castle of Bolton during the reign of James the Second: " He went to dinner at six or seven in the evening, and his meal lasted till six or seven the next morning, during which time he eat, drank, smoaked, talked, or listened to music. The company that dined with him were at liberty to rise and amuse themselves, or take a nap, whenever they were so disposed ; but the dishes and bottles were all the while standing upon the table." A contemporary, Abraham de la Pryme, in his MS. Ephemeris, says that he " pretended to be distracted, and would make all his men rise up at midnight, and would go a hunting with torch-light." This mode of living is said to have been affected by him in order that he might be thought unfit for public affairs at a time when things were going in a manner of which he did not approve. The Marquess put off his folly and appeared in his true character of a man of

Richard Shuttleworth, Mr. Dean of Ripon, Mr. Darcy, and others, there.

13. I went in the Marquess's coach to Richmond, accompanied with Mr. Cradock and all the officers of his court, and many of the Aldermen, and after supper at Mr. Cradock's, was attended by Mr. Mayor and his brethren, as also by Sir John Lawson,[a] Mr. Collingwood, Mr. Darcy, and many others, who came to bid me welcome to Richmond.

14. I preached at Richmond, and after dinner confirmed Sir Marmaduke Wyvil and about 300 more in that church; was entertained by Mr. Mayor and his brethren, and by Mr. Yorke, at his house. Received a letter from the high commissioners concerning clandestine marriages, which Mr. Cradock took a copy of, and I sent to the Dean of York a letter to signify my receipt of that circular letter.

15. I was accompanied by the gentlemen of Richmond to Peirsbrig, and met at Farewell Hall by some prebends and other gentlemen, and so conducted to Durham, where I was welcomed by the Dean and Prebends, Mayor and Aldermen, and many other gentlemen, who supped with me that night at Mr. Mickelton's.

16. I dined with Mr. Dean, and supped with Alderman Duck.[d]

17. I received 20 guineas of the Dean and Chapter for my books relating to the state of the college: delivered up my treasury books, and received a release under seal. Dined with Dr. Bagshaw then in residence, and supped at the castle with Mr. High Sheriff and his lady, and Dr. Montagu and Mr. Basire, and others.

---

sense and spirit when there was a prospect of saving the country from the effects of James's policy, as has been observed in a former note.

[a] Of Brough, the second Baronet.

[b] Of the rise of this remarkable person, afterwards Sir John Duck, there is a curious account in Sir Cuthbert Sharp's " List of the Knights and Burgesses that have represented the County and City of Durham in Parliament," 4to. 1831, p. 37.

18. I was at morning prayer, and took my leave of Mr. Dean and Dr. Grey, &c. and gave institute to Gabriel Blakiston, master of arts, to the rectory of Danby Wisk, alias Danby super Wisk cum Yatherton, and had Sir William Blakiston the patron's bond to save me harmless, after which I went to Peirsbrig accompanied by Sir Ralph Cole and others to Sunderland brig, and met at my inn by Sir Robert Eden and Mr. Brass.

19. Mr. Ralph Grey, M.A. of Christ's Coll. in Cambridge, and made priest by the Bishop of Lincoln, now curate of All Saints in Newcastle, came recommended to me by Dr. Grey and others for the title of chaplain, to qualify him for the more favour in that place, which I promised to send him when I met with Mr. Callis, but after gave it him myself, and returned safe that night to Ripon.

20. I took my leave of Sir Edmund Jennings in the evening, and supped with Mr. Francis Wyvil, and sent letters to my daughter Alicia, Sir Edmund Wiseman, Mr. Thomas Shepard, Mr. Towres, and Mr. Kidder, Mr. Salisbury, and Mr. Holmes. A bill of £22 sent to my cousin Wiseman from Mr. Wiseman, for my use.

21. I took my leave of my neighbours at Ripon after sermon, having dined with Sir Jonathan Jennings, &c.

22. I entertained Mr. Dean of Ripon, Mr. John and Francis Wyvil and his lady, and Mr. Mayor, at dinner, and after took my leave of the rest of my good neighbours.

23. I went from Ripon accompanied by Mr. Mayor and many of the aldermen and other gentlemen to Ripley, where being entertained by Sir John Ingleby,[a] Mr. Pomfret, and the minister of Nid, and Mr. Hodgson accompanied me to Leeds, where I supped with my brothers Milner[b] and Pemberton, and lodged at the vica-

---

[a] Sir John Ingleby of Ripley, the third Baronet, who went abroad with James the Second.

[b] The Vicar before mentioned.

rage, and was entertained by Mr. Hickes by the way, who supped with us.

24. I came safe I thank God through bad ways to Elland, where I lay, and Mr. Ashton accompanied me from thence, and my Lord Halifax's steward Mr. Turner, to Blakiston Edge.

25. I came over Blakiston Edge to Rochdale, where I was accompanied by Justice Butterworth of Bellfield, and two Mr. Hortons, and Mr. Pigot the vicar and his son, and many others, who accompanied me to Bury, from whence, 26 Nov. I went through Bolton, where the vicar, Mr. Lever, and others, met me and accompanied me over the moors to the Ferry's inn at the 4 Cards [*sic*] in Hilton, where my son John and Mr. Callis, Mr. Peake, and Mr. Turner, curates of Wigan, met me.

27. I came to Wigan before noon, was met 3 miles off by the mayor and aldermen, and several neighbouring gentleman; and at my entrance into the town was saluted with an elegant speech in Latin, and as well delivered, by Mr. Shaw the schoolmaster; after which, having visited the parsonage house, to which they accompanied me, and sealed a mandate to Mr. Peake to induct me, I returned to the church, was inducted, and heard morning prayer, after dined with some of my brethren of the clergy, was presented[a] and visited by the mayor and aldermen, Mr. Standish, Sir William Gerard,[b] and several other gentlemen, then went to evening prayers in my own chapel. I granted or confirmed what my predecessor had done under hand and seal, to John Laithwaite, the sexton's place of Wigan, *quamdiu se bene gesserit*. I sealed a letter of attorney to Mr. John Tickell of Whitehaven to be my attorney to gather my rents in Cumberland. I delivered Mr. Collis Mr. Gabriel Blakiston's presentation to Danby Wisk, and his subscription, &c. and Sir William Blakiston the patron's bond to save me

---

[a] What is to be understood by "presented," will appear in the notice of what passed on the second of December, when the Bishop arrived at Chester.

[b] The fourth Baronet.

harmless, and ordered him to send the curate of Leeds word (who is presented since by my Lord Baltimore) that the church is full, and he must take his course at law.[a]

28. I preached at Wigan, and read the prayers and Thirty-nine articles, and my son John preached there also in the afternoon. Was presented by several of the mayor, aldermen, &c. and recorder, who dined with me; and their wives waited on mine at night.

29. I went from Wigan towards Chester, accompanied by the mayor and aldermen, and my brethren of the clergy, and lodged at Frodsham; from whence I was conducted, 30 Nov., by the high sheriff and governor, and a great train of the gentry on horseback, and ten coaches, into the city, the guards drawn up from the gates to the palace, and was visited by most of the gentlemen and ladies about the city.

December.

1. I was sung into the cathedral by the choir in procession, and enthroned by Mr. Dean, and sung back into the palace after prayers. The warden of Manchester and three other clergymen dined with me and Mr. Brookes; and I made a visit to the governor of the castle, with Sir John Arderne and Mr. Dean, in the evening.

2. After prayers and sitting in the consistory, Sir Rowland Stanley, his brother Francis, Mr. Egerton, Sir Philip Egerton, and Mr. Chomley, and ten other gentlemen, dined with me; and after dinner the mayor and aldermen brought me a present of 8 sugar loaves, 1 dozen of canary, 1 doz. of white wine, and 2 of claret, and were merry with me till 7 at night, and many ladies visited my wife.

3. Dr. Allenson brought me Mr. Richard Legh's nomination, and had a license from me to officiate at Newton Chapel, upon Dr. Sherlock's recommendation, in whose parish it lies. Captain

---

[a] Gabriel Blakiston continued in firm possession of the living of Danby Wisk till his death in 1701, so that Lord Baltimore either abandoned his claim or was not able to enforce it.

Fielding and his son in law, and the subdean and archdeacon, and four other clergymen, dined with me, and my wife was visited by the governor's lady, Mrs. Walberton, and 10 more.

4. I wrote Serjeant Jefferson word that I would renew two lives and change the third, in the moiety of the rectory of Wallesey, to Mr. Edward Wilson, for £80 and an hogshead of claret, to be paid to Mr. Towers. I wrote to Major-General Worden, of making Mr. Stringer, of Nantwich, my surrogate. The schoolmaster and usher dined with me. Mr. Massey visited me before, and the Governor, Captain Fielding, and Mr. Anderson, after prayers.

5. I preached and received the Sacrament at St. Peter's in Chester; had Mr. Callis and his family, Mr. Peake and his wife, and two of the prebends and Mr. Hilton, at dinner; and visited by the recorder, governor, and two other of the officers at night, and my wife by my Lady Calverley, &c. I heard Dr. Fogg preach, and was at evening prayers in the cathedral.

6. I wrote to my cousin Peter Whalley of making my cousin P. Haddon curate of Wigan, at £40 per ann. and the perquisites of a reader, and cousin P. Whalley apparitor general, and to Mr. Holmes, to whom I sent an offer of Patrick Brompton for £80, and a dispensation for non-residence of Daniel Pinner, rector of Deane in Cumberland, because he was in a consumption; to H. Bulstrode and Jo. Ashton, Peter Haddon, Mr. Pemberton. I took the oaths at the Quarter Sessions in Chester, which were adjourned to this day for that purpose. I discharged Mr. Peake from attending the cure of Wigan any longer than till Christmas, because he is vicar of Bowden. The governor, recorder, Sir Thomas Grosvenor, and Dr. Angel, dined with me.

7. Mr. Hunter, one of the king's preachers, came to visit me, and Captain R. Graham. Mr. Massey sent me a doe. The parishioners of Childwel brought me Mr. Ambrose his resignation, and I promised to present a new vicar before Christmas; and wrote word to my cousin Peter Whalley that I would give it to my cousin Thomas West.

8. I wrote to Sir John Worden, and my cousin Flesher; to Mr. Bell; Mr. Ambrose resigned Childwel to me before the parishioners, and I accepted and signed the resignation. Mr. Oldfield and Mr. Cholmley, now high sheriff, visited me, and I went with my wife a visiting all the afternoon.

9. Mr. Mayor and his wife, and Mr. Sherwood, Mr. Hancock and his wife, who sent me a skeg of sturgeon, Mr. Callis et uxor, Mr. Dean, six captains, Mr.   , Mr. Warrington the brewer sent me twelve bottles of wine, and a sugar-loaf weighing 20lbs. After dinner Mr. Bridge, Alderman Willcock, Mr. Vanbrooke et uxor, and two daughters, and Dr. Pennington, came to visit me. I visited Sir John Arderne and his lady. Mr. Dean sent me a cheese. I wrote to the Bishops of Durham and Litchfield.

10. Mr. Gerard minister of Tarvin, and Mr. Garencieres minister of Warton, dined with me and Mr. Dean. After dinner we waited on my Lady Calverley, Mr. Subdean and Archdeacon, and Dr. Angel.

11. Mr. Warrington and his wife dined with me. We visited my Lady Warberton before prayers, in which time Sir Thomas Grosvenor and Colonel Whitley [a] came to have made me a visit, and the governor and his lady supped with us at Mr. Callis's.

12. I wrote to Mr. Cradock, Mr. Shepard, Mr. Bolstred, and Mr. Greswold. Mr. Archdeacon Allen [b] preached in the cathedral a very good and seasonable sermon. Mr. Shaw recommended Mr. Sumner (Alderman Scott's son of Wigan) to succeed Mr. Thomas Turner for reader there, which I granted if of age. Sir John Arderne brought Mr. Ravenscroft, Alderman Wilson, and the Recorder, to me in the evening.

13. I went to Sir Thomas Grosvenor's to dinner, where I had

[a] Roger Whitley, who had been a Colonel in the army of Charles the First, was seated at Peel Hall in Cheshire, where he entertained William the Third subsequently in his progress towards Ireland.

[b] John Allen, Archdeacon of Chester, Fellow of Trinity College, Cambridge, author of several printed Sermons.

an excellent entertainment. Sir Rowland Stanley, Sir John Arderne, and three clergymen there ; and at night supped with Sir John Arderne and Mr. Dean.

14. Mr. Dean, Mr. Wright, prebendary, Mr. Hancock, minister of St. Michael's, Dr. Percival, rector of Harden,[a] Dr. Pennington and Mr. Langford dined with me, and Sir Philip Egerton [b] brought his son after dinner, M. A. of Brasen-Nose Coll. with a good testimonial from them, dated in August last, to be made a Deacon next Sunday, twenty-four years old. Mr. Chancellor brought his lady, and Mrs. Wright. I received a letter from Mr. Legh of Lime, that his chapel could not be ready for consecration till my return from London because of the Lord Derby's being there, who is patron of Wigan and must consent to it. And another satirical letter from Mr. Peake, which I answered, and wrote to Mr. Ashton and the Lord Douglas.

15. Mr. Gabriel Stringer, minister of Nantwich, sent me a cheese weighing 80lbs. Sir James Powel [c] and his lady sent to see how we did, and would have come but that he had got a fall. Mr. Dean and Dr. Fogg's [d] curate, Mr. Wods, Mr. Vanbrooke, Mr. Daxon, dined with me. Mr. Edward Allen, vicar of Newton, sent me a firkin of Newton ale. Col. Whitley and his son Mr. Mainwaring came to visit me.

16. Mr. Richmond, minister of Sephton, Mr. Subdean et uxor et filia, and Mr. Jennings, dined with me. After dinner came Captain Fielding and his lady, Mr. Gleg and Mr. Allcourt, and Mr. Massey, visited me.

17. I wrote to Serjeant Jefferson in answer to Mr. Wilson's, about the lease of tithes. I received a warrant for a fat doe from

[a] Beaumont Percival, rector of Hawarden in Flintshire, from 168? to 1714.
[b] Sir Philip Egerton, of Oulton.
[c] Possibly for Poole.
[d] Laurence Fogg, who was ejected from the living of Hawarden for nonconformity in 1662 ; but afterwards conformed, and in 1672 was made vicar of St. Oswald's, Chester. He succeeded Arderne as dean in 1691, and died at a very advanced age in 1718.

my Lord Rivers. Several clergymen dined with me, who came to be ordained; and the governor and Alderman Wilcox stayed to supper with me.

18. My wine came in from London. I wrote to Dr. Paman to make Mr. Thomas Waite a public notary, and give my duty to his grace. Mr. Stephens, chaplain to Bishop Otway,[a] dined with me. I confirmed three to be made deacons in my private chapel after evening prayers, and gave a public admonition and exhortation to all who were to be ordained next day. Mr. Archdeacon and Mr. Dagget supped with me.

19. My son, Mr. John Cartwright, preached in the cathedral, after which I ordained

Deacons.

1. Ottiwell, Joh. A.B. Eman. Coll. cum literis dimissoriis ab Episc. Litchf. et Testimon. Coll. & from Mr. Hillen, Hudson, and Andrewes. Age 23.

2. Galley, Sam. A.B. S. Joh. Cant. Testimon. Coll. and from Mr. Hayes, Shaw, & Oakes. Age 25.

3. Smethurst, Rob. A.B. Jesu Coll. Cant. Testim. Coll. Age 23.

4. Dagget, Wm. A.B. Sidn. Coll. Testim. Coll. Age 23.

5. Hough, Edm. Jesu Cant. Testim. Hough, Turner, Moseley. Age 23.

6. Brereton, Wm. A. B. Jesu Cant. Testim. Coll. & Whittingham, Kent, Hayes. Age 24.

7. Thompson, Joh. Pembroc. Aul. Cant. Testim. Colby, Lancaster, Alcock. Age 25.

8. Basset, Tho. Col. Christi Cant. Literæ dimissor. ab Episc. Litchf. Testim. Shaw, Chetwin, Unton. Age 23.

9. Milnes, Jam. Joh. Coll. Cant. Testim. Oliver, Cole, Wood. Age 24.

---

[a] Dr. Thomas Otway, Bishop of Ossory.

10. Radley, Rich. Testim. Dean Arderne, Mr. Thompson, Gerard. Age 23.

11. Shelmerdine, Joh. A.M. Magdal. Coll. Cant. Testim. Coll. Mr. Waterhouse, Turner, White. Age 27.

12. Egerton, Phil. A.M. Œnei Nasi Oxon. Coll. Letters. Age 24.

Priests.

1. Haigh, Jam. A.B. Jesu Cant. Testim. Mr. Leigh, Savil, Jackson. He preached an excellent sermon at S. Oswell's in the afternoon. Age 26.

2. Liversedge, Jam. A.B. Magdal. Coll. Cant. Literæ dimis. ab Dec. et Capit. Ebor. Testim. Halley, Thomlinson. Age 25.

3. Barnard, Rob. A.B. Regin. Coll. Cant. Testim. Milner, Medcalfe, Benson. Age 24.

4. Lancaster, Tho. A.B. Trin. Coll. Cant. Coll. Letters. Mr. Coleby, Dr. Mason, Sir Medcalfe Robinson. Age 40.

5. Bolton, Edm. Testim. Mr. Brownsword, Zac. Taylor, and Burchale. Age 30.

6. Pocklington, Charl. A.M. Joh. Coll. Cant. Testim. Coll. Age 26.

7. Marsden, Chr. A.B. Joh. Coll. Cant. Mr. Thornton, Stable, Useden, Milner. Age 24.

8. Bethel, Tho. A.B. Nov. Hosp. Oxon. Mr. Symons, Waldron, Essex. Age 26.

I gave licence the same day to John Thompson to be curate of the chapel of Hardrow in Aisgarth.

I gave a licence to Rich. Radley to be curate of Tarvin.

I granted Sir Henry Herbert such a seat in Warth church as Sir Richard Graham and Dr. Samwayes should appoint.

I wrote to Sir Edward Blacket, Sir Medcalf Robinson, and Dr. Mason. Sir John Arderne and his lady, &c. supped with me, and Mrs. Ravenscroft.

20. Mr. Callis and Mr. Archdeacon dined with me. Mr.

Newcomb, rector of Tatnall, gave me a visit, and Col. Whitley sent me a doe.

21. Mr. Thomson preached in the cathedral, and I confirmed about 200. After dined with the Governor, Sir John Hanmore,[a] and Dr. Pennington, and my Lord Delamere's gentleman, supped with me.

22. Mr. Bradshaw, rector of Thurstaston, dined with me. I gave him a note to the Chancellor to provide him a parish clerk ; and Mr. Paine the merchant and I sign'd my son John Cartwright an instrument to be my chaplain. The deputy Register and my cousin West supped and lodged with me, and went the next morning to Childwall.

23. Sir John Crew,[b] Col. Whitley, Mr. John Mainwaring, the Governor and his lady, Dr. Angel et uxor, Mrs. Hudleston, Mr. Dean, and Sir John Hanmer, Mr. Shaw, and three other commanders, dined with me. Mr. Newton sent me an old cheese, the best I ever tasted.

24. Mr. Bowcher, Mr. Hancock, and Mr. Ru . . . r, dined with me, and Mr. Dean supped with me.

25. I preached and administered the Sacrament in the cathedral at Chester. Mr. Dean and the organist and vergers dined with me, and Mr. Anderton supped with me.

26. Mr. Dean preached. He and Mr. Anderton and his wife and two daughters dined with me. The Register and Mr. Dean supped with me.

27. I gave Mr. Thomas Waite, aged 24 years, his oath of public notary, by a commission sent me from Dr. Henry Paman, master of the faculties, dated 23 instant, and returned the commission certified under my hand this day. Mr. Hanmore preached and dined with me ; so did Mr. Attorney General, Alderman

---

[a] The third baronet of his family, then serving in parliament for Flint. He was a major-general, and afterwards distinguished himself at the battle of the Boyne.

[b] Of Utkington in Cheshire. He became a staunch supporter of the Revolution.

Wilcox, Mr. Wright, the Register, Mr. Callis and his daughter, and Mr. Tooke.

28. Mr. Thompson preached; Mr. Brookbanke, Mr. Chancellor, Mr. Register, &c. dined with me; Mr. Haddon and Mr. West came after prayers; My Lady Warberton and her daughter.[n]

29. I sealed a patent of the rural deaneries [?] in Chester to my son John Cartwright and Thomas Waite at £100 per annum rent. I sealed my cousin Peter Haddon, A.M. faculty, to be my chaplain. I sealed a licence to Jonathan Rutter to be schoolmaster in S. John's in Chester. Mr. Horton and Mr. Hulton, Mr. Dean, Mr. Chancellor, and Sir James Poole, dined with me and my cousins Haddon and West, and they and Mr. Recorder supped with me.

30. Sir Thomas Grosvenor and his lady and another lady, the Lady Warberton and her son and two daughters, Mr. Davis of Frodsham, dined with me; and the aldermen's wives were there after noon, and Mr. Warberton and Mr. Massey stayed to supper.

31. Mr. Wilcox, Dr. Pennington and his son, visited me, to whom I promised a licence to practise physic.

January 1687.

1. Mr. Hancock preached, and I confirmed about 350 persons. Dined at the Recorder's with Dr. Angel et uxor, Mr. Booth et uxor, Mrs. Lister, Mr. Chancellor et uxor, Mr. Loutherick, Sir John Hanmore. After supper I found Mr. Keeling at the palace.

2. Mr. Archdeacon preached. He and his landlady, and Mr. Callis and his children, dined with me.

3. Mr. Sherwood visited me, and presented me with a large cheese. I dined with the Lady Warberton, and was visited at night by my Lord Delamere and Col. Whitley, where we had

---

[a] Diana, daughter of Sir Edward Bishop, Baronet, of Parham, in Sussex, widow of Sir George Warburton, of Areley; buried at Chester 1693.

much discourse about [his and my Lord's . . . .
. . .].

4. I went to Mrs. Allford's funeral in the morning, and after
to Sir James Poole's to dinner, where I was kindly treated and
lodged that and the next night, with Sir Thomas Grosvenor et
uxor, Sir Rowland Stanley et uxor, Mr. Peters, Mr. Fitzharding,
Mr. Poole, &c. Mr. Massey, Mr. Dean.

5. We dined at Sir Rowland Stanley's, and returned at night
to Sir James Poole's, Mr. Babthorp [his priest with us].[a]

6. We went (all but Sir Thomas Grosvenor and his lady[b] and
Mrs. Rigby) to Mr. Massey's to dinner, and returned with him
that night to Chester, where he did us the favour to take a lodging
with us. Mr. Latham, Pr. and Mr. Kemp, alias Osbeston, P. dined
with us.[c]

7. Mr. Massey dined with me, and Mr. Wilkinson of Boroughbridge, and a young clergyman, Mr. Clarke, his neighbour, and
Mr. Recorder,[d] Mr. Norris, the Register, and Mr. Callis, supped
[with me; and after supper Mr. Massey came to me again, and
discoursed with me concerning poor Sir Thomas Grosvenor's
carriage to his wife, and her resolution to enter into a monastery
if he did not alter speedily, and consult her reputation and his
own better than he did.][e]

[a] Sir James Poole was the head of the Roman Catholic family of Poole, of Poole, in
the hundred of Wirral. Sir Rowland Stanley was another Cheshire baronet, seated in
the same parish of Eastham, at Hooton, and also a Roman Catholic.

[b] There seems to have been a reason for this which will appear afterwards. The Mr.
Massey, at whose house the bishop dined, must have been the neighbour of the Pooles
and the Stanleys, Massey of Podington, the head of another of the great Roman Catholic families of the hundred of Wirral, probably William Massey, who appears in one
of Mr. Ormerod's pedigrees (Cheshire, vol. ii. p. 309), father of the last of the name at
Podington, who was engaged in the Rebellion of 1715, and dying soon after left his
estate to the Stanleys of Hooton.

[c] Who seem to be two Roman Catholic Priests.

[d] Richard Levinge was at that time recorder of Chester.

[e] Sir Thomas Grosvenor was the third baronet, served the office of mayor of Chester
in 1685, and was at this time member for the city. He was thought to be favourable to

8.   I wrote to my Lord Peterborough, Mr. Polton, and Mr. Wilson.   Sir Thomas Grosvenor, Mr. Wilkinson and his friend, and Mr. Kent, dined [with me; and in the afternoon Sir Thomas Grosvenor and my Lady discoursed all those matters and causes of difference, and agreed upon these terms, that Mr. M.[a] should come to his house at any time when he was in the country, and be entertained as others, and that if any servants carried any tales between them on either side, they should be turned away; and that no public discourse of religion should be suffered in this house, but my lady be permitted to enjoy hers in private, she not writing to Mr. M. but what, upon request, she should shew to Sir Thomas, and what return he made her; and so Sir Thomas and my lady and Mrs. Rooksby, who, with my wife and daughter Sarah, were auditors of the whole matter, supped together with great satisfaction to all parties.]   My lady brought us a cheese.

9.   Mr. Hancock, who preached, Mr. Brookbank, Mr. Wilkinson and his friend, and Mr. Callis, dined with me; and the Governor came after dinner, and Mr. Philips, who now waits upon my Lord Montrath, and was servant to the Archbishop of York.

10.   A seat in the church of Liverpool, upon Mary Hesketh's resignation, granted to David Poole, merchant, and his heirs.   A

the designs of the King, and held a commission for the command of a troop in the Earl of Shrewsbury's regiment of horse, and was promised by the King, in a private audience, the regiment and a peerage if he would support in the House the Bill for the repeal of the Penal Laws against the Papists, and the Test Act.   But he refused, " preferring," as says the Peerage from whence these facts are derived, "the religion and liberty of his country to all honour and power, so likely at that time to be attended with popery and slavery."   His lady, it appears, had different views.   She was the sole daughter and heir of Alexander Davies, of Ebury, esquire, and brought the large property in the city of Westminster to the Grosvenor family, which is now possessed by them. Davies-street has its name from this family.   They married in 1676.   Sir Thomas died at the age of forty-three in June 1700.   Of the history of his lady, after his decease, there are some romantic particulars, if they can be relied upon, in that singular farrago the Collectanea of Colonel Colepeper, now in the Harleian department of the Museum Manuscripts, particularly in vol. ii. and vol. vii.   She went abroad.

    [a] Massey.

lease of Kirkby Ravensworth let to Sir Edward Blacket and Andrew Perrot for three lives, of Anne Jackson, Anne Cholmley, and Andrew Wilkinson. The two first were in the lease before, and for putting in the last I received £114. 18s. 8d.; and if the glebe and park and mortuaries be not included in the lease of £140 for the rectory, he is to pay a year's value of them more; he to repair the chancel, and to pay rent yearly £25. 5s. 4d. I wrote to Sir Edward Blacket about the rest of the fine. Letters to Mr. Hodgson, Sir Edmund Wiseman, Mr. Thomas Shepard, my Lord of Canterbury, and Dr. Paman, about Mr. Callis's lease. Mr. Wintringham dined with me and Captain Sanderson. I licensed Mr. Samuel Hulme to be curate of Knutsford, to which he was nominated by the Dean and Chapter of Christ Church, Oxon. 3 Jan. 1686. Sir Thomas Grosvenor, Mr. Recorder, Mr. Mayor, Alderman Wilson, Alderman Sparke, Lieutenant Win, drank with me, and Mr. Mayor invited me to dinner on Thursday next.

11. I received news of the parliament's prorogation to 28 April. Mr. Wintringham took his leave of me for Ireland. Mr. Chancellor and his brother Wright dined with me; Mr. Massey of Coddington, Mr. Ottey, Mr. George Becket, vicar of Eastham, was with me to desire payment 8 years at Childoe. Mr. William Francis, postmaster, dined with me also.

12. Mr. Hancock dined with me, and in the afternoon came to visit me Dr. Shippon and the high sheriff's chaplain, and supped with me.

13. Sir Peter Shakerley gave me a visit, and we dined with Mr. Mayor; Sir Thomas Grosvenor, Sir James Poole, Mr. Chomley, and Alderman Wilson, and the two sheriffs, and Mr. Anderson, were there. Sir John Arderne visited me, and Sir Thomas Grosvenor. I gave institution to Mr. Peter Needam to the rectory of Taxall. Mr. Massey, Sir James Poole, and Sir Thomas Grosvenor supped with me.

14. Sir Peter Shakerley, Sir Rowland Stanley, Sir James

Poole, and his uncle, Mr. Anderson, and Mr. Hilton, dined with me, and Mr. Pickering, Sir John Arderne, and Mr. Brooks, sat with me after prayers.

15. I wrote to cousin Mason, John Barnard, and Mr. Flesh-burne, and stated my accounts with them, and sent them two rentals, of Lincoln to cousin Mason, and of Beckeway to Mr. Flesh-burne, and desired them to mend what mistakes they found in them. Mr. Bourchier dined with me; Col. Whitley, and his three daughters, and Mrs. Angel and Sir Thomas Biddulph and Mr. Mainwaring were with me after noon, and Mr. Hancock from Mr. Allford to ask me forgiveness [for some ill reports he had made of me before my coming to Chester, which he was now con-vinced were false and groundless.]

I had advice of the Earl of Tyrconnel's resolution to lodge with me on Monday night.

16. I invited the Lord Tyrconnel by letter to the palace, sent by Sir J. P. Dr. Fogg preached. I sent the King's drops[a] to Mr. Allford, and invited C. Hamilton and his lady, &c. to dinner. Sir James Poole, Mr. Mostin, and the Recorder, dined with me. Mr. Hamilton and his lady, the Governor, visited me after prayers, and Dr. Foly and Mr. Massey supped with me.

17. I went 3 miles out of town in my coach to meet the Lord Tyrconnel and his lady, and took them into my coach, and he was received by the governor and soldiers, and conducted to the palace, where he and his lady lodged; there supped with them two Irish Lords, Col. Hamilton et frater, Mr. Molineux, Mr. Sheridon, Sir Rowland Stanley, Sir Thomas Grosvenor et uxor, Mr. Bab-thorp, Sir James Poole, Mr. Poole, Mr. Munston, Mr. Massey, Mr. Latham, pr. Sir John Hanmore, the Governor and his lady, Mrs. Sanderson, Capt. Fielding, Capt. Mackenzie, and all the officers of the garrison. The mayor and aldermen made him a present of wine, &c. The Chapter met him at the gates.

---

[a] A medicine so called. Mr. Allford died before the close of the month.

18. After breakfast I waited on my Lord and Lady, and conveyed them in my coach out of the city, where the governor and officers and I took leave of his Lordship going for Holywell. After prayers Mr. Herle came to me from Wigan, and acquainted me that Mr. Keeling had given bond of £1000 to answer the profits of Wigan to the successor; and he desired leave for Mr. Leigh to build a gallery in Wigan church, according to the grant made by my predecessor, to which I readily consented. My Lord Tyrconnel left 5 guineas to the servants. There were three Mr. Butlers with him. Sir James Poole, his lady, sister, and daughter, Sir Rowland Stanley and lady, Mr. Kemp, Mr. Dean, and five more, dined with me, after which we went in the same company to Sir Thomas Grosvenor's to supper.

19. We were nobly entertained at Sir Thomas Grosvenor's, with Sir Rowland Stanley and his lady and daughters, Sir James Poole, &c. Mr. Babthorp, and Mr. Kemp, and Mr. Poole, Mr. Massey et soror.

20. I went from Sir Thomas Grosvenor's in my own coach to prayers and the spiritual court in Chester, and returned thither to dinner, where I found, besides the former company, Mr. Peters, Mr. Mosson, and Mr. Brereton. I sealed Thomas Waite's patent to be a Proctor.

21. I came from Sir Thomas Grosvenor's with Sir Rowland Stanley, his lady, and Mr. Massey, and his sister, and Mr. Babthorp, who dined with me. I wrote to Major-general Worden. Mr. Boardman gave me a visit, and desired my assistance to reform an abuse of a charitable use in Grapnall. I went after dinner to Col. Whitley's, where I supped with Sir Michael Biddulph and his lady, Mr. Mainwaring and his lady, and Dr. Angel and his lady, Mr. Gerard, vicar, Mr. Radley, schoolmaster, and Mr. Vart, the colonel's chaplain.

22. I dined with the same company, and Sir Thomas Bellott and Mr. Bruen, and his brother of Stapleford, and supped there.

23. I preached at Tarvin, and confirmed about 90 persons, and

was entertained by Col. Whitley at a great dinner in the hall, which held 44 persons, among which were Sir John Arderne, Sir John Crew, Mr. Cholmley of Vale Royal, Mr. Dean, Mr. Recorder, Mr. Clapton, prebendary of St. Asaph, Mr. Sherwood, Alderman Mainwaring, Alderman Street, Mr. Hardwear and his wife and daughter; and the supper was also very great.

24. I went from Col. Whitley's to dine with Sir John Crew, where dined Sir Thomas Stephens et uxor, Sir Fr. Norrice' sister, Major Done's daughter, Sir Michael Biddulph, Sir John Arderne, Sir Thomas Bellot, Col. Whitley, Mr. Mainwaring, Mr. Sherwood, Mr. Hanmore, vicar of Waburham, Mr. Clapton, Mr. Dean, Mr. Vart, Mr. Colley, Dr. Foley, Alderman Mainwaring, and Alderman Street, Mr. Minshall, Mr. Callis. We supped at Mr. Cholmondeley's at Vale Royal, with Sir Thomas Grosvenor et uxor, and Mrs. Rigby, Mr. Oakes, vicar of Whitegate, Mr. Colly, and Mr. Callis.

25. I confirmed at Whitegate church about 300 persons, and returned to Vale Royal, where dined with me Sir Thomas Grosvenor et uxor, and Mrs. Rigby, Sir Philip Egerton, uxor et filius, Mr. Leftwich Oldfeild, Mr. Dean, Mr. Woods, vicar of Over, Mr. Marbury, rector of Davenham, Mr. Hanmore, Mr. Oakes, curate of Astbury, Mr. Oakes, Mr. Colley; and at supper Captain Birch and Captain Mainwaring more.

26. We returned with Sir Thomas Grosvenor et uxor to Chester to dinner, and after prayers Mr. Archdeacon, Mr. Thane, and Sir John Arderne and Mr. Walmsley of Leland came to visit me, and he delivered me a petition for the restoring of Euxton chapel to the inhabitants, the key whereof was in the hands of the Lord Molineux, who alledges that it is his and not theirs, that it has no maintenance, nor any prayers said in it for 20 years last past.

27. There dined with me Captain Carvell, Mr. Clopton, and Mr. Allenson of Newton. After dinner Mr. Babthorp brought

[me a paper of his thoughts on the question I put him when he was with me.]

Sir John Hanmore, Mr. Hilton, Sheriff Partington, Mr. Hilton of Hanmore, Mr. Horton of Leverpoole, who moved for a seat in the gallery there, in order to which I directed him to take out a citation, &c. against all opposers: and I gave the Register order to cite a schoolmaster who teaches without license to the prejudice of an honest man already settled in the parish of Weverham, recommended to me by Mr. Thomas Cholmondeley of Vale Royal.

28. I licensed Gabriel Dawson, priest, to be curate of Pilling chapel, in the parish of Garstang, in Lancashire, and John Farington, deacon, to be curate of Hulme chapel, in Sambach chapelry. I gave Mr. Samuel Shaw of Wigan a licence to teach the free school of Warrington. Colonel Whitley, Sir Michael Biddulph, and Mr. Mainwaring, gave me a visit.

29. I wrote to my Lords of Canterbury and Durham, Dr. Walgrave, Dr. H. James of Queen's, br. Stow, Bp. of Lincoln. I admonished Mr. Ottway, the precentor, in the church, of his neglecting services and anthems, and his teaching of the quire; and he refusing to amend, and be the packhorse, as he called it, to the quire and choristers, I told him I should take care to provide a better in his room, and one that should attend God's service better, and pay more respect to his superiors, he behaving himself very insolently towards the subdean at that very time. Sir Thomas Grosvenor dined with me. Mr. Booth, my Lord Delamere's uncle, and his son, came to visit me.[a] Mr. Massey supped

---

[a] Lord Delamere, whose name occurs in other places of the Diary, was Henry the second Lord, who was subjected to much political persecution in the reign of James the Second, and having been forward in promoting the Revolution was created Earl of Warrington in 1690. Of his uncle, Nathaniel Booth, who was seated at Mottram St. Andrew, little is known. When the heirs in the line of the peerage were exhausted, the title of baronet, which had been conferred on this family at the first institution of the order, revived in the descendants of this Nathaniel, but in a short time expired.

with me, Sir Thomas Grosvenor, and Mr. Recorder. I received a letter from my worthy friend and brother Thomas Bishop of Lincoln, by which he promised to give my son John the prebendary [a] of Leighton ecclesia in the church of Lincoln, now void.

30. Mr. Wright preached in the morning, and dined with me and Mr. Bolsworth from Ireland, and Dr. Fogg, in the afternoon. The governor came to visit me.

31. My son John went towards Lincoln to take possession of his prebendary. I wrote to Sir Richard Allibon, Bishops of Lincoln and Lichfield, Mr. Skelton, the Dean of Lincoln, cousin Peter Whalley, Mr. Ashton. Mr. Morrey preached in the cathedral, and I admonished him to mend his prayer, in which he gave not the King his titles, and to be wary of reflecting so imprudently as he did upon the King's religion, which he took thankfully and promised amendment.[b] Sir Thomas Grosvenor, Mr. Subdean, and Mr. Morrey supped with me, and Sir John Arderne and his lady, &c. came after supper. I wrote to my uncle Campion.

February.

1. I went with Mr. Allford's corpse out of town; returned to morning prayer. Mr. Massey dined with me and supped. I wrote to Lord Langdale [c] by Sir Thomas Grosvenor, and to my Lord Peterborough. My books were brought into the palace.

2. I was at St. Oswald's church, where Mr. Wood preached a commemoration sermon. Mr. Booth, Mr. Hancock et uxor, and another petty canon, dined with me. We supped at Mr. Chancellor's.

3. I sealed a patent of the apparitor-general's office to my sons

---

[a] So the word is written. It should be prebend.

[b] This clergyman was probably Peter Morrey, the Dean's curate, to whom he left his best gown, cassock, hat, silk stockings, and other articles of apparel. *Ormerod*, vol. ii. p. 40.

[c] Marmaduke, the second baron, Governor of Hull.

Gervas and Richard for their lives, which was confirmed by the Dean and Chapter.

4. Dr. Angel and Dr. Wroe dined with me, and Sir John Arderne visited me.

5. Mr. Waite brought his wife to Chester.

6. Dr. Wroe preached an excellent sermon on the King's inauguration, which I requested him to print, as highly seasonable.[a] He and Mr. Allen and Mr. Thane, and Mr. Ware and his son from Ireland, Mr. Callis and my cousin Waite and his wife dined with us, and after prayers we went to the governor's to celebrate the solemnity of the castle; and Dr. Wroe went with us, from whence we returned to supper. [I gave the gunners 5 shillings.]

7. Dr. Fogg and his wife and daughter dined with me, Mr. Booth, his wife, daughter, and sister, visited me. Mr. Chancellor's lady, Mrs. Gerard, Mrs. Wright, Mr. Bowcher, and Mr. Massey supped with us.

8. Mr. Massey, Mr. Chancellor, Mr. Wright, Mr. Davis, Mr. Kent, Mr. Callis, Lady Grosvenor, and Mrs. Rigby dined with me, who went after dinner with my wife and daughter to the horse-race; and at night I visited Sir John Arderne, where I found his eldest son and his nephew Arderne.

9. Being Ashwednesday, I preached in the cathedral at Chester to a very great congregation. Was visited by Captain Hungate in his passage to Ireland, Mr. Francis, Mr. Prescot, and Dr. Foley, and Mr. Peake supped with me.

10. I was in the consistory, and Mr. Venables dined with me, and Mr. Thompson, Mr. Newcomb, Mr. Waite et uxor, Mr. Callis. I gave a license to Thomas Wilson, B.A. deacon, to be curate of Newchurch in Winwick, upon Dr. Sherlock's letter. My Lady

---

[a] Dr. Richard Wroe, a prebendary of Chester, and at this time Warden of Manchester, a very excellent and popular preacher. He was a favourer of the Revolution. In the wardenship he had succeeded Dr. Nicholas Stratford, who had resigned it, and who subsequently succeeded Cartwright in the bishoprick of Chester.

Warburton and her daughters visited me, the Lady Calverley, Mrs. Warburton, Mrs. Cholmley, her sister, and Mr. Cholmondeley's daughter.

11. Madam Kightley came to Chester, and Dr. Haselwood and several more of my Lord Clarendon's family.[a] Mr. Cholmondeley came to visit me. Archdeacon Allen preached and dined with me. Dr. Haselwood the Lord Clarendon's chaplain, Mr. Cholmondeley, and Sir J. Arderne sat with me at night.

12. I sent my son Gervas up to London a deputation to sign for the apparitor general's place to   . I wrote to the Dean of Ripon and Mr. Risdel. Sir John Arderne and Dr. Haselwood sat with me at night.

13. I preached in the cathedral at Chester, being the first Sunday in Lent, to the greatest congregation that ever I saw, a sermon of Repentance. God give a blessing to it! Mrs. Cholmondeley and her sister and his daughter my Valentine,[b] and Mr. Warburton and his wife, and Major Car dined with me, and visited me again after prayers. I rebuked, as they deserved, Mrs. Brown, Mrs. Crutchley, Mrs. Eaton, and her sister, for talking and laughing in the church: and they accused Mr. Hudleston for being as guilty as themselves,

14. We dined with Mr. Warburton and his lady, where were Mrs. Cholmondeley, her sister, and daughter, Major Car, Mrs. Peake. After prayers Mrs. Dodd and Mrs. Fogg visited us.

15. There dined with me Mr. Brookes, Mr. Clopton, a doctor of physic, and after dinner Mrs. Cholmondeley and her company came to visit my wife, and Mr. Cholmondeley and the high sheriff, who supped with us.

[a] They were returning from Ireland where the Earl of Clarendon had just surrendered the vice-royalty to the Earl of Tyrconnel. Lady Frances Hyde, a daughter of the first Earl of Clarendon, married Thomas Kightley, Esq. of Hertingfordbury in Herts, who filled some office in Ireland under his brother in law the lord-lieutenant. For Dr. Haselwood, the chaplain to the earl, see Wood's *Fasti.*

[b] This was the vigil of the feast of St. Valentine. Pepys often speaks of his Valentine.

16. I wrote to Mr. Coles of London, to Sir Thomas Fanshaw, and Sir William Holcroft; Dr. Haselwood, the Lord Clarendon's chaplain, preached. Mr. High Sheriff and Mr. Francis Cholmondeley, Mr. Stringer, dined with me. I gave a license to Mr. William Vaudry to be curate of Church Hulme. Mr. Hide chaplain of Manchester, Sir Jeffery Shakerley and the Governor, and Sir John Arderne came in to visit me.

17. Mr. Hyde and Mr. Stones were with me, and Mr. Farindon, who gave up his former license and returned to his cure at Wettenhall. I admonished the inhabitants of Hulme Chapel in the consistory of their riotous shutting up the chapel doors on 6 Febr. being Sunday, the king's anniversary day of inauguration; and enjoined them penance for the same to be performed and certified against the next court day. There dined with me Mr. Poole and Mr. Cotterell of Backford, and Mr. Peter Leigh of Alford. I granted Mr. Hugh Poole a license to supply the chapel of Nether Peover, to which he was nominated by my Lady Leicester. I supped with Mr. Cholmondeley and the High Sheriff and the Lady Frances Kightley and Dr. Haselwood at Sir John Arderne's.

18. My cousin Haddon, cousin West, and cousin Stafford, Mr. High Sheriff, Mr. Cholmondeley, and Mr. Thompson, who preached, and Mrs. Dod, Dr. Haselwood, and two ministers more dined with me. I gave institution to my cousin Thomas West to the vicarage of Childoe, and made him my chaplain. Dr. Angel and his wife, and the governor's lady and sister, gave me a visit.

19. Sir Rowland Stanley, Mr. Oldfield, Mr. Ashton, and my cousin Stafford dined with me, and at night I admonished the ministers to be ordained to-morrow, of their duty.

20. Mr. Thane preached the ordination sermon in the cathedral at Chester, after which I ordained

Priests.

1. Alexander Ewart, A.M. Coll. Baliol. His testimonials from Mr. Whitle, Gerard, Wright. Age 30.

2. St. John Bingley, A.M. Coll. Glascow. Testim. Mr. Spencer, Eaton, Betton. Age 25.

3. Jonathan Stafford, of Wolston, cum literis dimissor. ab Episopo Litchfield. Testim. Mr. Whaley, Harris, Hutchinson, Draper. Age 38.

4. Richard Weaver, A.B. Coll. Ænei Nasi. Testim. Dr. Shippen, Mr. Beadsley, Mr. Newton. Age 26.

5. Jonathan Lawrence, A.B. Coll. Sid. Cant. Literæ dimiss. ab episc. Litchf. Testim. Mr. Dolman, Scot, Jordan. Age 25.

6. Henry Woods, A.B. Ænei Nasi. Testim. Mr. Penny, Mallory, Fichwicke. Age 26.

7. William Brereton, A.B. Jesu Cant. Testim. Coll. Whittingham, Kent, and Hayes.

Deacons.

1. Robert Solden, A.B. Coll. Div. Johan. Cant. Testim. à Collegio. Lit. dimissor. ab episc. Litchf. Age 23.

2. Nathan Goulbourne, A.B. Coll. Magd. Cant. Test. Mr. Hyde, Boardman, Ward. Age 24.

3. Samuel Garrett, Coll. Eman. Cant. Testim. à Colleg. Age 23.

These all dined with me, and Mr. Minshaw the bookseller, the Lady Frances Kightley, and the Lady Arderne, Sir John, the Recorder and his lady, and Mr. Hide visited me at night.

21. I wrote to Mr. Andrew Wilson, vicar of Easingwold, to require the pension of £5 per annum to my cousin Peter Whalley, and Bishop of Lichfield. Dined at the Lady Grosvenor's with Mr. Godfrey. Was sent for from thence to meet my Lord Clarendon which I did with my wife, son, and daughter, 5 miles from Chester on the Sands, into which he was conducted to the deanery with all expressions of joy.

22. I conducted my Lord Clarendon through the cloisters to his seat in the church, from whence he went to dine at the castle.

Sir Paul Ricot,[a] Sir James Poole, Mr. Poole, Mr. Davis and his son, and Mr. Ware, dined with me. Sir Philip Egerton and Mr. Francis Cholmondeley came to visit me. I supped at night with my Lord Clarendon at the deanery, where was my Lord of Derby, the High Sheriff, Mr. Cholmondeley, and many other persons of quality.

23. I waited upon my lord to the cathedral, where Mr. Peake preached a sermon of the duty of governors, before my Lord Clarendon and Lord Derby, instead of a Lenten sermon. My Lord Clarendon and Bishop of St. Asaph, &c. visited me after evening prayer, and I supped with their lordships at Sir John Arderne's at night. I gave Mr. Ashton, in a letter, the account of my lord's reception.

24. After morning prayer I waited on my Lord Clarendon out of Chester. Received a visit from the Earl of Derby.[b] Mr. Massey returned with me to dinner. My Lord and Mr. Thomas Cholmondeley interceded for Mr. Peake's indiscretion.

25. Mr. Hancock preached an excellent practical sermon ; and he and his wife dined with me and Sir James Poole and much other company, Mr. Davis of Frodsham. At night the Governor and Colonel Daniel brought Mr. Peake to me, who made many frivolous excuses for his indiscretion, of which I gave him a severe admonition, and exhorted him to humility, and told him that I believed my counsel was in vain to a man of such pride of spirit and petulancy as I had found him before to be of, and that I would not have thrown it away upon him but at the persuasion of Mr. Thomas Cholmondeley, who requested me to try him once more, and that if he did amend 'twas beyond my hopes, and that I had withdrawn his license of preaching but for Mr. Cholmondeley's inter-

---

[a] Sir Paul Rycaut, the celebrated traveller and author of " The History of the Turks." He had been knighted by James the Second, and was Secretary for Leinster and Connaught during Lord Clarendon's Lieutenancy.

[b] William, the ninth Earl of the Stanleys. He was removed by James the Second from the Lord Lieutenancy of Lancashire.

cession, but upon his amendment he need not despair of my favour.[a]

26. I took physic and kept in my study all day, where I received visits from Major Car and other officers who were leaving this place, and in the evening received a letter from Sir Charles Porter [b] by his servant to borrow my coach from Nesson, when I heard of his arrival; which I cheerfully granted, and invited him to accept a lodging for himself and his lady at the palace, but was told by his servant that he had already bespoken them in the city, and promised that his son and what friends he had in town would dine with me to-morrow.

27. Mr. Porter, Mr. Simons, Mr. Yong, Mr. Hide, Captain Feilding, Captain Dalevil, and another of the new officers dined me. Mr. Thompson preached, and at night Mr. Recorder, Sir John Arderne, Col. Daniel, and two friends of his drank with me.

28. I wrote to Sir Alexander Fitton and Mr. Pemberton. Dr. Angel and his lady dined with me. Sir Standish Hardstone, Sir John Jacob,[c] Sir John Arderne, Col. Daniel and his priest, whom Sir John would importune me to commend to Wigan school, visited me.

March.

1. Mr. Paine dined with me. The recorder was with me in the evening.

---

[a] It cannot but strike the reader who is acquainted with the proceedings concerning Magdalene College, Oxford, how strongly this address to Mr. Peake resembles the rebuke which the bishop thought it his duty to give to the refractory fellows of that college. The King also himself spoke of " Humility," to persons whose just rights he was secretly undermining, or openly invading.

[b] He was the Lord Chancellor of Ireland in the year 1686, and appears to have been now on his return to England. His successor, Sir Alexander Fitton, was appointed on February 12 in this year. (See *Beatson*, vol. ii. p. 211.) He was made a peer by James the Second after his abdication.

[c] The third baronet of his family. He afterwards served with credit in Ireland in the command of a regiment under William the Third.

2. Mr. Wood preached an excellent sermon of charity in St. Oswald's church. He and Mr. Edwards and Mr. Oakes dined with me; and Mr. Callis, Mr. Wright came after to visit me.

3. I was in the consistory, and determined at night a cause of defamation by a summary hearing between Allenson and a boatman. The Chancellor, Register, and Mr. Allenson supped with me. I dined at Mr. Booth's[a] with Lady Frances Kightley.

4. Dr. Fogg preached an excellent sermon of Repentance. He and his wife and daughter, and the schoolmaster, dined with me. In the afternoon I determined the case of Congleton by a summary hearing in my study; allowed it to be a burial place, they paying their duties as is particularly mentioned in the license, to the mother church of Astbury, with which both parties seemed well satisfied, Mr. Egerton, the subdean and archdeacon being by.

5. I sent my coach after dinner to Nesson to fetch Sir Charles Porter and his lady to Chester, which found his children set in a stage coach, broke in the quicksands, 3 miles from Chester, and having brought them back, went forward again to fetch Sir Charles and his lady against to-morrow morning tide.

6. I preached and delivered the Sacrament in the abbey. Sir Charles Porter and his lady, children, and friends, my Lady Frances Kightley and hers, Mr. Taylor and his lady, Mr. Limeing, Sir John Arderne and his lady and son dined with me; and after evening prayer Sir Charles Porter and the governor came up into my study with Sir John Arderne, from whom I went with my wife, son, and daughter, to the Lady Grosvenor's, where I met Mr. Goeden.

---

[a] This Mr. Booth, with whom the Bishop dines, is not to be confounded with the Nathaniel Booth before mentioned, the uncle of the first Earl of Warrington. The Mr. Booth intended is George Booth, eldest son of Sir John Booth, a younger son of Sir George the first baronet. This George Booth was a lawyer and prothonotary of the county palatine of Chester. He is the author of a Treatise on Real Actions, and also of a Translation of Diodorus Siculus. He died in 1719 at the age of 84, and was buried in St. Oswald's church, Chester.

7. I continued at Eaton, dined with my Lady, who after dinner carried my wife, son, and daughter to the race, and returned to me at night with Mr. Goeden.

8. I continued at Eaton, where dined with us Mr. Goeden and his brother, Sir James Poole, Mr. Poole, who after dinner went to the race; but I continued in Sir Thomas Grosvenor's study till night.

9. I returned in the morning by seven to Chester; Mr. Davis he preached. He and his wife, my Lady Grosvenor, Mr. Goeden, Mr. Massey, cousin West, dined with me. Mr. Hulmes came to me after dinner, and Sir Charles Porter's lady to take her leave, after prayers, and Mr. Massey and I placed my pictures in my library, the Durham goods coming up that morning.

10. After prayers I sat in the consistory, and decreed the seats in Nantwich to Mr. Cholmondeley, and another seat wholly to Mr. Yates and the vicar Faulkner for life, of which Mr. Peter Yates had formerly the half; he having now two or three other seats in his possession in the same church, which he calls his freeholds under his hand, and ordered his kinsman to repay him his £5 with which he says he purchased his freeholds, to which he pretends this half-seat to be annexed. Mr. Anthropos dined with me. Mr. Pocklington came to ask leave to church, christen, and marry and deliver the sacrament in the lady Leicester's chapel, which I denied to give him, because not consecrated. Mr. Dean was with me at night. Mr. Holcroft came to my service this day at £10 per annum.

11. Mr. Newcomb, rector of Tadnall, preached a most methodical and practical sermon, which I desired him to print for the public good, but he modestly waived it: he dined with me and Mr. Colly. After dinner Colonel Hastings, Sir John Jacomb,[a] and Captain Herne visited me.

12. A French Protestant minister dined with me from the Bishop of St. Asaph, and Mr. Key and Mr. Boucher.

[a] Thus in the MS. but probably intended for Sir John Jacob mentioned before.

13. Mr. John Bowker preached. The Lord Mountjoy [a] was at church with many other officers. Mr. Cartwright and the preacher dined with me. After prayers the Lord Mountjoy, Mr. Cootes, the Governor, Major Hastings, Captain Dixy, Mr. Delavil, and Mr. Taylor sat with me three hours, and Mr. Taylor supped with me.

14. After evening prayer I went to visit Mat. Anderton, who had been ill; and whilst I was there, the governor, a Scotch captain, and Sir John Parker came in, from whence I returned to supper.

15. Col. Whitley and the Lady Calverley came to visit me in the afternoon.

16. Mr. Hulme preached an ingenious sermon of the wisdom of being religious; he and my Lord Mountjoy and Colonel Makarty, Mr. Coot, Major Hastings, and Mr. Callis dined with me, and Mr. Taylor, Dr. Pennington, and his son, visited me.

17. I was in the consistory, after which, Mr. Chancellor, Mr. Oldfield, and Mr. Babthorp, came and dined with me, and Mr. Massey visited me and Mr. Lutwich Oldfield.

18. My cousin West dined with me, and we went to visit Mr. Recorder's lady, Mr. Warmingham, and Mat. Anderton, where we met Mr. Massey, who came home with us.

19. Sir Rowland Stanley and his lady, and Mr. Babthorp, Sir James Poole, brother and uncle, Mr. Kemp, Mr. Massey, Captain Bierley, Captain Dixey, Captain Salisbury, dined with us.

20. Mr. Archdeacon Allen preached an excellent and seasonable sermon, and he and Mr. Thane dined with me. I went to visit the Lady Warburton and the Governor. Mr. Shaw and Mr. John Sumpner supped with me, and I gave Mr. Sumpner a license to be schoolmaster of Wigan, upon the feoffees' presentation.

21. Dr. Angel and Mr. Dean dined with me, and after Sir John came.

[a] The first Viscount Montjoy of Ireland. He was a great promoter of the Protestant interest in that country.

22.   We visited Lady Calverley, Mr. Mayor, and Dr. Angel.

23.   I preached in the cathedral.   Col. Whitley, Mr. Mainwaring, Dr. Angel and his wife, and Mr. Brookes, dined with me;
and I licensed Mr. William Johnson to be curate of Garsdale in
Sadberge parish in Yorkshire.

24.   Mr. Thomas Cholmondeley and Mr. Oldfield dined with
me, and I ordered him his seat in the gallery at Manchester,
paying £2 4s. per annum to the chaplains, without arrears.   I
visited Madam Bridgman and the Lady Frances Kightley, and
sealed a patent of the commissaryship of Richmond, to Mr. Thomas Cradock and Mr. John Cartwright.

25.   I preached and administered the Sacrament, being Good
Friday, in the cathedral; after which Mr. Dean and the Chapter
confirmed the patent I made yesterday of the commissary's place
of Richmond to Mr. Thomas Cradock and Mr. John Cartwright,
for their two lives; visited Mrs. Callis, Dr. Fogg, and the castle.

26.   Sir James Poole and his brother dined with me, and I
sealed a confirmation of Mr. Leftwich Oldfield's two seats in the
gallery at Manchester at 44s. per annum, and a license to Dr. Pennington's son to practise physic in Lancashire.   I took my leave
of Mrs. Walburne, Mrs. Booth, Mrs. Dod, Mr. Anderton, Sir John
Arderne, and the recorder, with whom at the archdeacon's we discoursed who was to pay the archdeacon's elect Michaelmas rent.

27.   I was at the cathedral and delivered the Sacrament. After
dinner Mr. Thane, Mr. Callis with us, Sir John Arderne, the Governor, and Alderman Wilcox went to prayers with us in our private chapel: after which we went to Col. Whitley's, where we had
a noble supper with Mr. Mainwaring, Mr. Dean, Dr. Angel, Mr.
Vart, Mr. Trevers, Mr. Gerard.

28.   We went from the Colonel's to Nantwich, where we dined
at the post house with Mr. Stringer, Mr. Mainwaring, Mr. Wil-
burham, the churchwardens, and two officers; and from thence we
went that night to Stone, where Mr. Hall and Mr. Massey met
us, and I wrote to Mr. Franklin concerning Mr. Bradley, vicar of
Stone.

29. We went from Stone to Sir Michael Biddulph's,[a] where we had a noble dinner; after which we went to my uncle Hutchinson's at Litchfield, with whom we supped and lodged, and broke our fast next morning; his two sons and daughters, Mr. Baker, and Mr. Nicholson, the register, being with us.

30. We went to Sir John Bridgman's to dinner, where we met his son Lloyd, and were very nobly entertained; from thence we went to Litchfield, where we met my aunt Haddon, my cousin Stafford, honest Mr. Hutchinson, and Mr. Holliland, his son in law, and my brother Knightley's man, with a kind invitation to Charleton. We supped with the Bishop of Litchfield, and lodged at the Star.

31. We dined with the Bishop, and after went to Charleton, where we was very kindly entertained.

April.

1. I went in Mr. Knightley's coach to see the school and church of Preston, and was at the master's, rector's, and Mr. Butler's house, from whence I went to Fawsley, where Mrs. Knightley and her son bid me heartily welcome, and accompanied me back to Charleton to dinner, where Mr. Bourchier and Mr. Wright met us, and Mr. Sherwood, who brought us part of the way towards Northampton, where we were met by my cousin P. Whalley, Daniel, Mr. Ives, and his brother, Mr. Gardiner, Mr. Cockeram, &c.

2. I went to visit Dr. Conant,[b] my cousin Gardiner, Mr. Archer, Mr. Lovel, dined with Mr. Wentworth at my cousin Ives'; was visited by Mr. Freeman, Sir William Langham, Mr. Fleetwood, &c.

---

[a] Sir Michael Biddulph the second Baronet. His name has occurred before. His wife was one of the daughters of Colonel Whitley, so often mentioned.

[b] John Conant, Vicar of All Saints, Northampton, Prebendary of Worcester, and Archdeacon of Norwich. He had been Rector of Exeter College, Oxford, and Vice-Chancellor of that University. Died in 1698, aged 80.

3. I preached and administered the sacrament at Allhallows in Northampton, where they all came up upon my invitation to the altar, who had never done it before, except Mr. Cockeram and Mr. Clarke, the former of which spoke more than became him, and refused to come up to take satisfaction to his scruple, clapped on his hat and went out;[a] God forgive him, and bring him into the way of truth. After evening sermon we were treated at Mr. Lovell's, and returned to supper, where we met Mr. King the curate and other friends. After dinner Mr. Mayor and his brethren brought me up a dozen bottles of wine, and returned me thanks for my sermon, and condemned the rudeness and factiousness of Cockeram and Clarke, and desired it might not be imputed to the prejudice of the corporation, who were and always would be ready to conform to all to which the Doctor should invite them.

4. We took our leaves of my cousin Ives, called at Sir John Holman's,[b] dined at Coocknoe with my cousin P. Whalley, cousin Ives, Nathaniel and his wife, Daniel; and after dinner went to Billing to visit the Earl of Thomond;[c] and returned to supper, where we met my cousin Welsh.

5. We dined and supped at Coocknoe, where Mr. Archer and Mr. Palmer came to visit us, and another minister with him.

6. We took our leave of my cousin Whalley, and a little beyond Dainton[d] our axletree broke, which occasioned our stay there 3 or 4 hours, and we went that night to Hockley in the hole, where Mr. William Duncomb sent us six bottles of claret.

7. We dined at the Mitre in Barnet, where Mr. Cleave, a

[a] The custom of taking the sacrament kneeling was not generally insisted upon in towns where, like Northampton, there was a strong infusion of Puritan feeling. This was a part of the ritual of the Church of England to which the Puritans had a strong aversion.

[b] Of Weston-Favel, younger brother of George Holman of Warkworth, in the same county.

[c] Henry O'Brien the seventh Earl; of the Privy Council to Charles the Second and James the Second. He died at his seat of Billing in 1691.

[d] Thus in the MS.; probably Daintree is intended.

clergyman, met us; from thence we came to the King's sadler's against the Mews by Charing Cross, and that night I visited my Lord Peterborough and Major-General Worden, and kissed the King's hand in the bed-chamber before supper.

8. I was at the King's levee, and as his Majesty brought the Queen in to dinner, she was graciously pleased to offer me her hand to kiss, and as his Majesty went to council in afternoon, he called me to him in the gallery, and appointed me to attend him in his closet the next day in the evening. That morning Sir Thomas Grosvenor, who had delivered up his commission the night before, came to me for satisfaction, whether in [conscience he] could submit to the taking off the penal laws, to whom I read my papers, with which he declared himself well satisfied, but that he thought the king expected the taking off all penal laws, &c.[a] I met Captain Byerley and C. Fairfax. Dr. Thompson came to me at night, and Mr. Ashton, &c. I dined with my Lady Peterborough and Bernard Howard, where we discoursed the business of the Duchess of Norfolk.[b]

9. Mr. Clayton was with me in the morning, and Mr. Galford, with whom I went to the Bishop of Rochester, and from thence to Lambeth to dinner, where I stayed evening prayer, and after attended his Majesty in his closet for an hour, where I was received very graciously, and had his promise of being kinder [to me upon all occasions, and being well satisfied with the services I had done him in] my diocese. I recommended the Governor and Colonel

---

[a] See the preceding note respecting the behaviour of Sir Thomas Grosvenor.

[b] Lady Mary Mordaunt, the only child of the Earl of Peterborough, was married in 1677 to Henry the seventh Duke of Norfolk of the Howards. A little before this time he separated himself from her, not, as appears, without cause; but it was not till 1700 that he obtained an Act of Parliament for dissolving the marriage and enabling him to marry again. The Duke died in the following year, and the Duchess then married Sir John Germaine. Bernard Howard, who was at this conference, was the eighth son of Henry Frederick Earl of Arundel. His posterity have succeeded to the honours of the family by the extinction of all the elder male lines, and now enjoy them.

Whitley [as a penitent, and one who would strive to deserve his favour for the time to come; and told him what papers I have given to F. Petre,[a] with which he was well pleased.] After which I wrote to the governor and Mr. Massey, and went to my old land-lady's, to Sir John Pettus,[b] and my Lord Stirling,[c] and his son my Lord Alexander.

10. I heard Dr. Stillingfleet at 7 in the morning in the King's chapel,[d] and Dr. Tillotson at 10, upon Moses by faith refusing to be called the son of Pharaoh's daughter, and choosing rather to endure affliction with the people [of God, than to enjoy the pleasures of sin for a season; who in the close magnified those who in this hour of temptation stick so close to the Church of England as to choose rather to be God's favourites than the King's, &c.[e]] I was at the levee. I dined at the Bishop of Durham's and my son with the Bishops of Rochester and Peterborough [to whom I gave an account of the Sacrament which I delivered at Northampton the Sunday before, and received his thanks for bringing them up to the altar.] I went to Sir Edmund Wiseman, returned and found him at my lodgings, who went with my wife and daughter into Hyde Park; and I sought Bishop Labourne; found [him not at home, but met the Irish archbishop, with whom I had a] long discourse. Saw Mr. Elstob and cousin Fletcher. I discoursed with F. Petre.

11. I was at the levee; received Burnet's libel [f] from F. Petre,

[a] The first appearance of this name. Father Petre was a priest who had great influence with the King, and was admitted by him into the Privy Council in 1688. The Bishop, it will be seen, was in frequent communication with him.

[b] Of Rackheath in Norfolk, the second Baronet; author of *Fodinæ Regales* and other works.

[c] Henry Alexander, the fourth Earl.

[d] Dr. Stillingfleet was at this time Dean of St. Paul's, and was afterwards Bishop of Worcester.

[e] Tillotson was at this time Dean of Canterbury. He appears to have had a distinct apprehension of the danger in which the Reformed Church of England was then placed.

[f] Burnet was at that time abroad. It is not evident which of the pamphlets attributed to him is the one intended.

and returned it; discoursed with Lord Huntingdon [a] about my
sister Barnard's concern and Bishop of Rochester. Mr. Clarke
visited me, and one from Sir John Lowther. I dined with my
Lord Mayor, Sir John Peake; met there Sir William Pritchard,
Sir James Smith, Sir John Shaw, and Mr. Backwell. From thence
I went to visit Sir Richard Allebon,[b] Sir Roger L'Estrange, Sir
John Lowther, and Bishop Labourne, and after visited the King
and Queen.

12. I waited on the King before dinner, was visited by my Lord
Antram,[c] Mr. Elstob, Mr. Clayton, and others. Dined at home
with my sister Barnard, Mr. Furnis and his son my landlord.
Wrote letters to Mr. Callis; Mr. John Hall brought me the King's
presentation to the vicarage of Anderby in Yorkshire, my diocese,
but directed to the Dean and Chapter of York. Dr. Dove was
with me. I spoke with the King in the gallery, and Mr. Ware. I
visited Sir Richard Allebone.

13. The King went a hunting, and dined with the princesses
at Richmond. Mr. Yarwood was with me about Knutsford. My
Lord Preston gave me a visit, and encouraged [me to put in this
time for York, by promising me the assistance of all his country-
men.][d] I waited on Colonel Mackarte, F. P. and Col. Worden,
and Mr. Shaw promised me a visit. Mr. Clapton came to visit me.
After dinner I went to see my cousin Backwell, Mr. John Cooke,
Lord Chief Baron and Lord Chief Justice Wright, and Sir Charles
Porter; and saw the King at his return.

[a] Theophilus Hastings, the seventh Earl of Huntingdon of that family. He was
divested, on the change of the times, of all the offices which had been conferred upon
him by King James, and was excluded from the benefit of the Act of Indemnity of
1690.

[b] Soon afterwards made one of the Judges of the King's Bench.

[c] So in the original; but probably Lord Ancram is the person intended.

[d] Archbishop Dolben died on the 11th. The see was kept vacant for more than
two years, a perpetual temptation to men of the spirit of Bishop Cartwright. The
filling it by Lamplugh, Bishop of Exeter, was one of the last acts of regal authority
performed by King James.

14. I was at the King's levee, and returning home I met Serjeant Jefferson, and my Lord Bishop Labourne gave me a visit [to whom I gave an account of the King's preachers in Lancashire, and desired him to acquaint the King with the condition of them, and I gave my Lord] Sir James Poole's snuff-box. I visited Charles Fanshaw and my Lady. Sir Richard Wiseman and sister Barnard dined with me. I went to Sir Benj. Thoroughgood's and met Sir Thomas Fanshaw; visited Dr. Beveridge, where I found Dr. Agar and Goodman; Lord Chief Justice Wright, where I met Sir Charles Porter.

15. I was at the King's levee; went from thence to Jenkins and Parslow, where I spoke heartily to Mr. F.[a] concerning an allowance to his son William, but not with so good success as I designed; supped and lay at Jenkins.

16. Before dinner I went to Mr. Walseye's; there dined with us at Jenkins, my Father Wight and Mr. Clemens, Mr. Bush, Mr. Fanshaw, and his son, came in after dinner. We visited Mrs. Streams at Uphall, and returned to Jenkins to supper.

17. I preached at Barking, and dined at Jenkins with Serjeant Winter[b] and Mr. Tison, and Mr. Fanshaw and his son.

18. I dined at my Father Wight's with my wife and daughter, and Sir Thomas and his lady and sisters, and Mr. Benjamin. I visited Mrs. Goddard, Mr. Chisnall, Mrs. Walsey, and returned to Jenkins.

19. I received a letter from my Lord Chancellor Jeffereys to attend my Lord President [c] and him at his house to-morrow at 12 of the clock, upon some business that concerned his Majesty's service. I waited on the King at dinner, and dined with my Lord Peterborough; went after dinner with the Bishop of St. David's to

[a] Fanshaw: Jenkins and Parslow were seats of this family.
[b] Thus in the MS.: but no Serjeant of this name is known.
[c] The Earl of Sunderland.

visit Sir H. Firebrasse [a] and his lady, and Mr. Rowland and his,[b] my Lord Bishop Labourne who was not within, my Lord Chancellor who received me kindly, and F. P. who was not within. I wrote to Mr. Dean, Mr. Massey, Mr. Mickelton, and Mr. Recorder of Chester.

20. I was at the King's levee, and spoke with Captain Conden, Captain Pack, Bishop of St. David's, Mr. Bidel, and Mr. Ashton. I received of Mr. Michael Wharton for Cottingham rent due at Martlemas £29 9*s.* Mr. John Hall instituted by me to the vicarage of Anderby and licensed to preach, and received for his fees due to my secretary £3 ; Mr. Francklin's clerk taking for his pains £1 10*s.* Sir Edmund Wiseman, Mr. William and John Fanshaw, Mr. William Coles and Mr. Crofts were with me. I met my Lord President and the Bishops of Durham, Rochester, Peterborough, and Oxon, at my Lord Chancellor's, where he and my Lord President, before dinner, acquainted us that his Majesty expected [thanks from us for the care he had of us, and the gracious promises he hath made to protect us in his late gracious declaration ;[c] of which] I penned the form, and with the Bishop of Oxon subscribed it before dinner, and carried it down to my Lord Chancellor, who after dinner asked the other three to do it, two of which, Rochester and Peterborough, refused [till the form of it were something] altered, which being done, Durham, Rochester, and I subscribed it; Peterborough desired to deliberate till to-morrow; and we were ordered to meet there again at 4 in the afternoon for that

[a] Sir Henry Firebrace, who had been much in the confidence of King Charles the First, and who, in the reigns of Charles the Second and James the Second, had an office in the household. His name frequently occurs in this Diary.

[b] *Sic.*

[c] The Declaration for Liberty of Conscience, published on the 4th of April. The matter which follows is peculiarly interesting, as presenting us with the secret history of the Bishops' address delivered on that occasion, so critical in the then state of parties. Not the least curious part of the information is that when the Bishop of Chester had penned a memorial of thanks to the King, he went immediately to Bishop Labourne, and on the next day to Father Petre, to report what had passed.

purpose. [Rochester and Peterborough said, they could not but remember how vehemently the King had declared against toleration, and said he would never by any counsel be tempted to suffer it. My Lord President replied; though they could not choose but remember it, yet they might choose whether they might repeat it or not, for other men as well as the King had altered their minds upon new motives. They both extolled the Bishop of London,[a] even to the condemnation of the King.] The Bishop of St. David's, Mrs. Elstob, and Sir Thomas Grosvenor came to me at night. My Lord of Durham and I visited Bishop Labourne.

21. I gave F. P. and the Lord Peterborough an account of yesterday's debate; attended the King at his levee, returned and discoursed Mr. Gatford, dined with the Bishop of St. David's, my wife, son, and daughter at Mr. Rowland's. Went to my Lord Chancellor's, where my Lord President told us the King liked well of our subscriptions, but the Bishop of Peterborough utterly refused to join with us.[b] I attended the high Commissioners to hear the Cambridge cause,[c] which was deferred until Wednesday

[a] Compton, one of the steadiest of the opponents of the measures of King James.

[b] Dr. Thomas White. He was afterwards one of the seven Bishops who presented themselves before the King with a petition that their clergy might be excused from reading the Declaration, when they boldly referred the King to the fact that the dispensing power had often been declared to be illegal in Parliament. Yet he as well as others of the seven Bishops, though they had stood prominently forward in this act as opponents of the measures of King James, could not approve of the removing him from the throne, and retired into private life rather than offend their consciences by taking the oaths to King William ; a great and memorable instance of mighty sacrifice being made at the call of conscience. Of the other Bishops who were present on this occasion, Crew and Sprat, though they signed the address, and were at least not active in their opposition to the measures of the Court in matters of religion, took the oaths to King William on the change of the times. Cartwright and Parker did not live long enough to be put to the trial.

[c] The King issued his mandate to the Vice-chancellor of Cambridge, Dr. Pechell, to admit to the degree of Master of Arts, Allan Francis, a Benedictine monk. Compliance was refused ; whereupon Francis summoned the Vice-chancellor to appear before the Commissioners for Ecclesiastical Affairs; and in the end he was deprived of his Vice-chancellorship and of the Mastership of Magdalene College.

next. Went to my Lord Chief Justice Wright, to congratulate
his removal to the King's Bench; with the Bishop of St. David's
and Mr. Rowland, where I met the Bishop of Peterborough. Returned and supped with my wife and sister Barnard.

22. I was at the King's levee, and after with the Bishop of St.
David's visited Sir Thomas Exton, and dined with Sir H. Firebrasse [there I met Bishop Labourne and my Lord Arundel, who
carried me into Father Gally's chamber to hear Capuchio sing;
from whence I visited Major-general Worden. Then went into
the privy council, where Mr. Thompson the lawyer engaged me to
be with him on Monday night, and Captain Seymore some night
next week; then I returned home, and from thence to the Bishop
of Oxon, where I met Dr. Elliot, who promised to bring me acquainted with Mr. Peepes.] [a]

23. I was at the King's levee; dined with Mr. Elstob with my
wife, son, and daughter, and Mr. Ridley and Mr. Ashton, and his
wife. Wrote to Mr. Dean, spoke with my Lord Marquess of
Powis [b] and the Lord President.

24. I heard both the sermons at Whitehall, was at the King's
levee, spoke with Mr. Molineux about Mr. West and my son, to
whom he promised a living if it fell. With my Lord Delamere,
visited Sir Roger L'Estrange, Sir John Lowther, and Mr. Molineux; Sir William Meredith, Dr. James, and the Bishop of St.
David's with me at night, and Mr. Pollen supped with me.

25. I was at the King's levee, heard the Declamations at Westminster School, dined with the Bishop of Rochester and the Elec-

---

[b] This is the uniform orthography of the name of Pepys as written by the Bishop,
and no doubt represents the manner in which the word was pronounced. It will of
course suggest at once the remarkable person whose Diary has afforded so much entertainment, as well as so much insight into the state of society, the manners and poli-
tics, of the reign of Charles the Second.

[a] William Herbert Earl of Powis, advanced to the Marquisate on the coronation of
James the Second, whose fortunes he afterwards followed, and died abroad in 1696.

tors, met my Lord President, Bishops of Durham and Rochester at my Lord Chancellor's, and subscribed an address to the King, which I sent down to the Bishops of Lichfield and Lincoln, the Deans of York and Ripon and my own diocese the next day. Met Mr. Cooke and the Bishop of St. David's at Mr. Thompson's house in Essex Street.

26. I was at the King's levee; Captain Salisbury and Dr. Elliot visited me, the Lord Ancram, and the Bishop of St. David's. I dined with my wife and daughter, at Mr. John Ashton's, and supped at Captain Byerley's with Lord Preston and Mr. Wyn.

27. I was at the King's levee; was visited by Mr. Vane, who carried me into Hyde Park. There dined with me Mr. Ashton and his wife, Mr. Birch, Mr. Elstob, and his nephew, Mr. Clayton. I spoke at the Commissioners' hearing of the Cambridge business; with Sir Thomas Pinfold, and Mr. Peepes. The King spoke to me of the Bishop of Winchester.[a] Mrs. Streames, Mr. Rowland and his wife, dined with me. I supped with the Bishop of Rochester, and found Mr. Ware and Mr. Tucker at my lodging.

28. I received of Mr. Rice Jones for the year's rent of Langathern, due at Lady day last, £18 6s. 8d. I went to the King's levee, and from thence to the Parliament House, where I sat till the prorogation to 22 November. From thence I went to dinner with Sir Richard Allebone in Serjeant's Inn, who gave me a ring.[b] After dinner I delivered my privy seal to be instated in my first fruits of Chester, for the fees whereof Mr. Tucker gave me a bill of £18 10s. 6d. the clerk of the crown, of £6 for my first sitting in the House of Lords, and the chamber-keepers £1 demanded. Dr. Dove was with me, and refused to sign the address, first, [because not sent by the archbishop: I told him we had none, and I was his diocesan, as archdeacon. Secondly, because it referred to the declaration, for no portion whereof he could give

---

[a] Dr. Peter Mews, promoted by King James; but not concurring in his designs.
[b] This was the day of his call. Pointer, p. 342.

thanks, without owning himself obliged for the whole.]　I wrote to Mr. Callis, Mr. Dean, and Dr. Fogg.

29.　I was at the King's levee, saw the Quakers bring their address,[a] was with Father P.　Dined with my family and Mr. Taylor and Mr. Winwick, at Mr. William Coles.　Went to the Bishop of Oxon, where I received the Bishop of Lincoln's letter concerning his approbation and promoting the address to the King;[b] which I shewed after to his Majesty [in his closet, together with another letter from Mr. Massey, both which he highly approved of, and declared that such men as myself, who had always stuck to him, should never want his favour; and that he would take an effectual course to make others weary of their obstinacy.　And I advised him to begin with his own household, which he promised to do.]　I supped with my Lord Preston, Sir John Fenwick,[c] and Major Ramsey.

30.　Mrs. Gardiner the wax-chandler and Mr. Grey my chaplain were with me in the morning, and Mr. Prestwich's heir brought me a subpoena to appear on Tuesday at 2 of the clock in the Common Pleas at Westminster, to witness his will.　I spoke with Dr. Grey, Archdeacon of Buckingham, with my Lord of Durham, and carried my son and Mr. Grey to dine with me at Lambeth, where I met the Dean of Lichfield, to whom I shewed, as also the Archbishop and Bishop of D. and the Lord President, and Lord Powis, and F. Ellis, and Lord Langdale, the Bishop of Lincoln's letter, and to Sir Roger L'Estrange, who was with me.　I wrote

---

[a] Of thanks for the Declaration.　These addresses were general throughout the various denominations of Non-Conformists, to whom, with whatever intention issued, it practically gave relief from some very severe enactments of the preceding reign.

[b] This was considered a great point gained, as appears by what follows.　The Bishop of Lincoln at that time was Dr. Thomas Barlow, who, though favouring too much the measures of King James, found no difficulty, or at least made none, in taking the oaths to King William.　How much more dignified is the conduct of Sancroft and the pious and venerable men who thought and acted with him.

[c] Afterwards put to death for a plot against the life of King William.

to the Bishop of Lincoln, Sir John Duck, and the Marquess of Winchester, and gave Dr. Elliot a guinea for his advice to Jervas.

May.

1. [I was with Bishop Labourne, who conducted me into a convenient place in St. James's Chapel, where I saw] Monsieur Dada consecrated Archbishop of Amasea in Ponto, after which I returned home to dinner. I went to the Bishop of Oxon, and Whitehall, where I met Sir Richard Allebone, and went with him to Mr. Chiffin's chamber, where I met Sir Charles Porter and Topham.

2. I was at the King's levee before he went to Chatham; visited Major-general Worden, where I found William Pen;[a] returned home to dinner, where Sir Richard Wiseman and my cousin Whalley dined with me and sister Barnard. I sealed the bonds for the first fruits of my bishoprick. Visited Mr. Maydwell, Lord Aylesbury,[b] Mr. Loggan, Mr. Royly, met Mr. Robert Bertie, and called with Sir John Lowther upon Sir Roger L'Estrange. Mr. Clayton came to me.

3. I was with my Lord Chancellor about granting the curatorship of Sir Roger Bradshawe's children from Lady to Mr. P. Shakerley, because of her marriage, upon which he ordered both parties to attend him. I wrote to Dr. Hooke and Mr. Pemberton. Col. Whitley and Mr. William Fanshaw dined with me. I went into the Common Pleas to witness Mr. P. Prestwich's will. Mr. Pollen and Mr. Dolben visited me, and Mr. Willson, about the lease of Wallezy.

4. I was at Hackney, dined with Captain Fetherston at my Lady Wood's; visited my cousins at Limehouse, called on Dr.

---

[a] The celebrated Quaker, who was much about the King at this time, attended him in his progress in this summer, and when at Chester " held forth " in the open air, as the Bishop relates.

[b] Thomas Bruce second Earl of Aylesbury, a Catholic peer, who retired to the Continent on the Revolution, and died at Brussels in 1741.

Bridges and Dr. Beveridge, not at home. Was at Court, and supped at home.

5. I was at the King's levee, and with F. P. Wrote to Mr. Cholmondeley, Mr. Callis, Mr. Dean, Mr. Cholmondeley, and Dr. Fogg, and spoke with Mr. Bowes to write to Mr. Cradock. Mr. William Fanshaw and sister Barnard dined with me. I went with the Bishop of St. David's to Mr. Ridley to supper. He and Mr. Elstob returned with me.

6. This being the day of his Majesty's miraculous deliverance and escape out of the Gloucester frigate, which was sunk, I was at his levee, where he put Sir Ch. Scarborough in mind of the deliverance.[a] Dr. Forster, the chancellor of Lincoln, was with me, and promised to remind my Lord of my son John when any living fell, and to be register to his prebend. I read Dr. Fogg's letter and my answer to it to Lord Langdale, spoke with Sir Paul Rycott and Sir Roger L'Estrange. My cous. Nath. and Peter Whalley were with me, and Mr. Apelford subscribed the address. I was to visit the Irish Bishop, and met the Archbishop.

7. My Lord Molineux his son came to take his leave of me, Bishop of Durham to visit me and Mr. Peirce the chirurgion, and Mr. Peake; and F. P. sent me word he expected me to-morrow, between 6 and 7. Two men from the Mayor and Aldermen of Preston to hinder the building of a gallery in their church to their prejudice. I attended the sentence of the Cambridge men before the high commissioners (after I had dined with Major-general Worden with my wife, son, and daughter), where the Vice-chancellor was deprived of his office and vote for ever after in any senate in the University, and suspended *ab officio et beneficio,* from the mastership of Magdalene during the King's pleasure, and the profits to go to the college; and rest of their representa-

---

[a] The Gloster was lost May 6, 1682, on her return from Scotland, when James, then Duke of York, was saved with difficulty. Sir Charles Scarborough, the court physician, was also on board, and had a very narrow escape. See for this Pepys's Correspondence.

tives to receive sentence on Thursday next, when I am summoned
to be at a court of delegates at 3 of the clock in Serjeants' Inn in
Fleet-street. I wrote to the Bishops of Chichester and Carlisle
and Mr. Callis, and Bishop of Lichfield and the Dean of Chester.

8. I waited on F. P. in the morning; preached and delivered
the sacrament at Serjeants' Inn in Chancery-lane, and dined
there; returned to prayers to Whitehall.

9. I was at the King's levee; Sir J. Lowther was with me.
Sir Thomas Fanshaw and his lady, and her sister and brother
Charles and William Fanshaw dined with me. I visited the
Bishop of Oxon.

10. I was at the King's levee; spoke [with him before dinner
about Sir R. L'Estrange his address and our own at Chester and
Lichfield; and was commanded by him to print the MS.] Dined
with Dr. Elliot at Mr. Peepes'.

11. I was seized with a great pain in my back. Sir Thomas
Williams and Mr. William Fanshaw dined with me. Bishop
Labourne visited me, and I saw the Irish Bishop.

12. I saw the King and Lord Powis before dinner. Cousin
P. Whalley and his wife, Mrs. Mayoress of Chester, and her son
and daughter, and Dr. Hollingsworth and brother Milner dined
with me. I went to the high commissioners, where the Cambridge men were dismissed with a severe reprimand, and bid to
sin no more, lest a worse thing befell them. Col. Philips was
made chancellor of the Duchy, and the Lord Powis promised my
son the chaplain's place to his son's regiment. I went with Mr.
Binion to visit Sir Thomas Maleverer, and paid Mr. Tucker 20
guineas for the privy seal for my first fruits, and his other pains,
and Sir Thomas Duppa £6 for my fees due to the officers attending the House of Lords at my first admission on 28 April last past.

13. I took physic. Mr. Goodin dined with me. Col. Worden
came to visit me. I went to Whitehall in the evening.

14. I was at Whitehall before dinner, and left Dr. Hooke's
Cassander translated with F. P. Dined with my Lord Hunting-

ton, visited [the] Bishop [of] Peterborough, Sir Thomas Exton, and Dr. Beveridge,[a] Dr. Crowder and cousin Grahâm. Wrote to Mr. William Willson and Dr. Hooke, Mr. Cholmondeley, and Mr. Dean.

15. I was at sermon at Whitehall. Dined with the Earl of Peterborough. Went to prayers in the evening. Spoke with F. P. about Dr. Hooke's book.

16. I dined with Mr. Sheffield, visited the Earl of Bath, Col. Phelips, and the primate, and Bishop Labourne; carried Sir Richard Wiseman to the King's bedchamber at night.

17. 1 was at the King's levee, and joined with the Duke of Beaufort in recommending Dr. Thompson to the prebend of Westminster, void by Dr. Sill's death,[b] who told me that if he had not promised it before to the Lord Barkley's son,[c] he should have it: if he had, he would be sure to remember Dr. Thompson in something else. I went with William Fanshaw to the Lady Peterborough, who approved and promised to promote his petition to the Queen; and spoke with Mr. East and Mr. B. . . ., and promised my Lord Preston to sup with him to-morrow night, and Captain Richardson to sup with him on Friday with Serjeant Jefferson. I visited Sir Thomas Meeres and his lady, Madam Dolben, and Mr. Shelden, the Bishop of Ely, Dr. Beveridge, Mr. Gatford, Dr. Hesketh, Dr. Bridge, and Col. Whitley, and wrote to Mr. Dean and Mr. Mickelton and T. Cradock.

18. The Primate of Ireland[d] and the Irish Bishop, Dr. Johnson,[e]

[a] Probably Dr. William Beveridge, Archdeacon of Colchester, who in 1704 was made Bishop of St. Asaph.

[b] William Sill, A.M. Archdeacon of Colchester.

[c] George Berkeley, the second son of George the first Earl of Berkeley, was made a Prebendary of Westminster in 1687.

[d] The Archbishop of Armagh at this time was Dr. Michael Boyle.

[e] Dr. Nathaniel Johnston, formerly a physician at Pontefract, but now retired from practice and living in London. He lent his antiquarian knowledge to the assistance of King James in the policy he was now pursuing, particularly in his work written to quiet the minds of those who might be apprehensive of the security of their title to

and Mr. Gatford and Dean of Carlisle,[a] came to visit me. Mr. Venables and Mr. Milner dined with me. I supped with my Lord Preston.

19. I was at the King's levee, who went this day to Windsor; visited Sir Thomas Maleverer; dined with Mr. Vane and Mr. Errington; visited the Lord of Durham, and went to my new lodgings in King-street in Covent-garden. Wrote to brother Barnard and Stow, and Dean of Chester.

20. Part of my goods came from Chester. I wrote to Sir Thomas Fanshaw. Supped with Serj. Jefferson, Sir Edmund Wiseman, my son, and Mr. Tempest, and Mr. Fairebeard, and Col. Enbruck [?] at Capt. Richardson's.

21. I wrote to the Bishop and Chancellor of Lincoln, and went to Sir Thomas Fanshaw's.

22. I preached and delivered the Sacrament at Barking, dined with Sir Thomas Fanshaw and supped with Mr. Chichenhall.

23. I dined at Sir Thomas Fanshaw's with my Lady Hyde and Sir William Holcroft, &c. and supped there.

24. I came up to London; went with Sir John Lowther and Sir William Holcroft to Mr. Medworthy, to Sir Richard Allebone's and my Lord Chief Justice Wright's.

25. I sealed two leases for lives of two tenements in York; one to Elizabeth Reyner for the lives of Roger Ward, Priscilla his wife, and Thomas Basto at £12 per annum; one life then void and the other two changed for 20 guineas; the other worth £2 per annum, 2 lives dead, for £8, to Mr. Roger Ward; the Secretary's fees for both to be accounted for by Mr. Ward of Furnival's Inn, as Mr. Callis received for the last. Dr. Johnson, Dr. Clarke's widow, my cousin Peter Whalley, his son, and nephew, Mrs. Musgrave and Mr. Bowes dined with me, and a petitioner of Queen's College Chapel came to petition for Over, which I declared to have given

abbey-lands acquired by their ancestors, and in his larger work in assertion of the King's visitatorial power over the Universities and Colleges.

[a] William Graham, afterwards Dean of Wells.

to Col. Whitley's chaplain, whom I collated to the same that afternoon, and received for his fees due to my secretary £3 10s. Mr. Franklin's clerk taking for his fees £1 10s.

26. I went to Windsor, was welcomed by the King, heard the sermon and music on Corpus Christi day, dined with the chaplains, visited Mr. Dean at night.

27. I was at the King's levee, who went a hunting. I dined with Dr. Sparrow, and supped with Fergus Grahame and the Dean of Carlisle.

28. I was at the King's levee, dined with Col. Grahame at Bagshot, and returned to the King's supper.

29. I was at the first sermon, and after at the King's levee, who ordered me to deliver my address at 10 after the rising of the cabinet council, which was graciously accepted, and answered with a speech of his Majesty's to this effect.—" My Lord, I could expect no less than such a loyal address as this from a prelate of such approved loyalty as you have been, and am fully convinced that, where my Bishops are loyal, the Clergy of the Church of England will easily be ruled by them in any thing relating to my service; and I do assure you and them that whilst they continue their duty they shall never find me unmindful of my engagements to them, but ready to make good all that I have promised them, and to stand by them as long as I live; but when the Bishops are wanting in doing their duties, I cannot but expect their clergy shall be unmindful of theirs." After this the Bishop of Peterborough, who was present in the crowd, came down to me to the second sermon, which was a very good one, preached by the Duchess of Monmouth's chaplain, and I dined at my Lord President's with the Lord Chancellor, Ailesbury, Godolphin,[a] Plymouth,[b] Sir Richard Allebone, Mr. Guy, Mr. Grandison, Mr. Abel singing

---

[a] Sydney the first Lord Godolphin, then a Commissioner of the Treasury.

[b] Thomas Lord Windsor, who had been created Earl of Plymouth in 1682.

all dinner time. I after went to Sir H. Firebrasse's and the Dean of Carlisle, and met Sir Richard Wiseman.

30. I was at the King's levee, who went a hunting, and I returned to London with Sir R. Wiseman and the Dean of Carlisle in my own coach. I dined with my Lord of Durham, and went to hear the exercises at Mr. Maidwell's school.

31. I waited on [the] Marquess of Powis with William Fanshaw; met the King at Whitehall; dined with the Earl of Pembroke; wrote to Mr. Dean of Chester and York, the Governor of Chester, Mayor of Wigan,[a] and Mr. Cradock, about addressing. I went to the Lord Privy Seal,[b] Sir Thomas Chichley's, Captain Paston's, and Sir Roger L'Estrange. Sir Edward Villiers and Dr. Elliot visited me.

June.

1. I bound my ungracious son Richard to Robert Peirce, chirurgeon, for five years, and gave with him £43, he to find him

---

[a] The Letter which the Bishop addressed to the Mayor of Wigan has found its way into the British Museum, and is now art. 37 of the Additional MS. 4164. It was pointed out to me by Mr. J. G. Nichols. A copy is subjoined as it shews the terms in which the Bishop's communications with the country were conceived.

      " Mr. Mayor,   May 31, 1687, London.

" I finding that the King expects Addresses from the several Corporations in the Kingdom as well as from the Clergy, and that he graciously accepts them, thought myself obliged to give you notice of it; and have accordingly sent you a form, which you may either subscribe or alter more to your own minds; not doubting but that you and the rest of your brethren, who have formerly been so eminent for your loyalty, will readily embrace this occasion of expressing your duty to God and the King, by which you will shew yourselves true sons of the Church of England, and oblige,

                  "Your affectionate friend to serve you,
                                    THO. CESTRIENSIS."

The art. 20 of MS. Addl. 4182, is a draft of the same letter.

[b] Henry Lord Arundel of Wardour, recently appointed.

clothes for the future. There dined with me Sir Thomas Fanshaw, Sir Jonathan Jennings, Mr. Lovel, cousin P. Whalley, Mr. Appleford, William Fanshaw, and F. Eubanke. The Lord Pembroke and Sir Thomas Chicheley and Mr. Cole were to visit me, and I to visit Mr. John Ashton and Mr. De Puy.

2. Dr. Samways and Mr. Weld, and Sir William Gerard, was with me in the morning, by whom I wrote to Mr. Richard Legh of Lime about the chapel consecration.

3. I went to Westminster Hall; visited Dr. Covel[a] and Mr. Dav. Lindsey, and dined with Dr. Comber at the Lord Preston's. Mr. Morgan came to see me.

4. I went to Westminster Hall, dined at the Knight Marshal's, Sir Edward Villiers, with Sir Jonathan Jennings, Dr. Elliot, and W. Etherich. Went to the physic garden and Chelsey college, where I met the Lord Mayor, and returned by Millbank. Wrote to the Bishops of Lincoln and Lichfield.

5. I heard Dr. Jeffrys preach at St. James's, received the Sacrament there; was visited by Sir William Meredith, his lady and brother, Sir William Dawson, and Dean of Durham.

6. Mr. Maleverer brought Mr. Ash to me for institution to Kirkby More. I went to prayers to Stepney, and brought my cousin Fr. Wingate and cousin Margaret home with me to dinner aud carried them back at night. Was visited by Lady Fanshaw, Charles and William, and Mr. William Booth. I was at Whitehall with the High Commissioners, where the Vice-President of Magdalene was asked by my Lord Chancellor whether he did not receive a mandate from the King to make Mr. Farmer president, and why he disobeyed it; to which he replying that he desired time to advise with counsel before he answers, his Lordship said that he was like a man of his coat (Ailworth[b] a civilian) first to do

---

[a] Probably John Covell, D.D. rector of Littlebury in Essex.

[b] This is another instance of the carelessness with which the Diary is written in respect to the orthography of proper names. The Vice-President of Magdalene College

an ill thing, and then to advise with counsel to defend it; but told him in fine, that the Commissioners would not be so hasty in adjudging him as he had been in disobeying and contemning the King's authority, and therefore, bidding him bring the statutes with him, gave him till Monday next. I spoke with the Lord President, the Lord Huntington, Bishops of Rochester and Durham.

7. I gave institution to Mr. Leonard Ash to the vicarage of Kirkby Moor, who left for my secretary's fees £3. I went to F. P. at Whitehall and to Westminster Hall, dined with my Lord Privy Seal, where I met Sir Edward Smith. Moved Sir Rowland Stanley's friend's business and Mr. W. Fanshaw's to F. P.; gave him the Chancellor of Lincoln's [a] letter to shew the King, having shewn it myself to the Lord Huntington; went to see Mrs. Montagu, Sir R. L'Estrange, Mr. Grahame of Clifford's Inn, where I met Barnard Howard, Sir Edmund Wiseman, and Baron Jenner, and the swordbearer, and waited also on the Lord Chief Baron Atkins.

8. I dined with Sir William Booth, went with him to the camp, where we met the King.[b] Went that night to Windsor, where I recommended his brother Booth of Allerton to the King's favour, and supped with Col. Nichols.

9. I was at the King's levee, and presented Mr. Allen with the Richmond address,[c] and procured the King's mandate to make him the next fellow of Trinity Hall. I dined with the Earl of Peterborough and the Lord Castlehaven. My good patron told me of some displeasure F. P. had expressed against me for reflecting [upon his . . . . . and wished me to be wary of those designing

was Dr. Charles Aldworth, who was conspicuously distinguished in the memorable stand of the college against the arbitrary act of the King. This is the first notice of the contest that has occurred in the Diary; but it will be seen that the Bishop of Chester went in a short time an Ecclesiastical Commissioner to visit the College in the King's name. Dr. Aldworth was elected in 1691 the Camden Professor of History.

[a] Samuel Fuller, afterwards Dean.

[b] The camp at Hounslow. "The King took great delight to be there every day in person." *Quadriennium Jacobi*, 12mo. 1689, p. 93.

[c] The Address from the Clergy of the Archdeaconry of Richmond.

people, and told me freely the present state of Northamptonshire.]
I returned to London that night.

10. I went to Westminster Hall, where I met Sir J. Lowther
and Mr. Stockdale, and Sir H. Benningfield, Mr. Dean of Durham,
Dr. Basire, Sir William Dawson, Mr. Gatford, and 3 or 4 Lincoln
. . . . . dined with us, after which came Mr. Drummond and Mr.
Elsley from Thomas Cradock, and I received letters from the Bishops of Lincoln and Lichfield, about the addresses [and one that
pleased me not from the governor of Chester, of his addressing,
in a better form of his own drawing.] Mr. Dean of Durham, Dr.
Basire, Dr. Eliot, &c. dined with me, and Sir Jonathan Jennings.

11. I went with Sir Richard Wiseman to Windsor.

12. I heard both the sermons at Windsor, and returned to
London at night.

13. I dined with the Bishop of Durham, and Mr. Charles and
Wortley Montagu and the Dean of Durham. Justice Warren
supped with me.

14. I dined with my Lord Ailesbury and gave him Dr. Forster's justification. The Chancellor of Lincoln came to me, and we
went to Justice Wright's.

15. I was at Westminster Hall in the morning, and Justice
Warren dined with me, and I received the Wigan address.

16. I heard Dr. Comber preach, and dined at Yorkshire feast,
and visited Sir Thomas Strickland and Lord Ancram. Mr. Stockdale and Dean of Durham supped with me.

17. On Friday I was a witness in Mr. William Cole's cause in
Guildhall. Visited Col. Whitley. The Bishop of St. David's and
Dean of Durham and Dr. Basire dined with me and Sir Richard
Wiseman, whom I carried to Windsor with the Wigan address;
having first visited Bishop Labourne, I spoke with the King that
night, and acquainted him with Mr. Barnard's lecture against his
supremacy, whom he promised to reprimand.

18. I delivered the Wigan address to the King; my Lord Ancram attending me, and his Majesty received it very graciously, and

gave great commendations of the constant loyalty of the Church of England, and renewed his promises of protecting it. I dined with the Dean of Durham and Sir Richard Wiseman at the Provost of Eton's, and visited the Bishop of Oxon, and was after treated at the Dean of Gernseye's very nobly, and Mr. Munstevens supped with me, and Sir Richard Wiseman, when I gave him the Bishop of Lincoln's letter to shew to my Lord President, and a book to give to the Lord Chancellor; of neither of which I have any account. I delivered one the night before to the King, which he graciously received, and gave to F. P. another, and Col. Philips.

19. I heard both the sermons at Windsor, and after them Mr. H. . . . in the King's Chapel, and excellent music; met my Lord Mayor and Lord Chief Justice there; dined with the chaplains; gave Mr. Dean of Chester's letter to F. P. to shew the King, from whom I am promised an account to-morrow of that and his Majesty's pleasure of my longer stay, and then returned with Sir R. Wiseman to London, who supped with me.

20. Mr. Thompson was with me in the morning. I visited my Lord of Durham, and dined after at Lambeth. I visited Mr. William Pen, and there supped with me Sir Thomas Fanshaw and his lady, and Ch. Fanshaw, Sir Richard Wiseman, the Bishop of St. David's.

21. I visited Sir Thomas Maleverer and Mr. Dupuy, Mr. Maleverer and Sir Jonathan Jennings dined [with me, to both whom I gave the] book. The Bishop of Durham and Lord Privy Seal, and B. Wood's lady, and 5 more visited me, and Mr. Elstob and Mr. Woodefield. I wrote to the Bishop of Lincoln and Mr. Dean of Chester. Mr. William Coles and William Fanshaw supped with me.

22. I visited F. P. at Whitehall, and after heard the Magdalene College business decided before the Commissioners, whose sentence was, that the Vice-President should be suspended from his office and Dr. Fairfax from his Fellowship, and President's place declared void; before which was given in the blackest character

of Mr. Farmer, for whom they received the King's mandate, that any modest man would blush to hear, and any on this side hell to be found guilty of it.[a]　Dr. Johnson dined with me.　I went to cousin Backwell's.

[a] This seems the proper place to introduce an outline of the Magdalene College affair, as far as it had then proceeded. A mere outline will be sufficient. Information having been received on March 31 of the death of Dr. Henry Clarke, the President of the College, the Vice President, Dr. Aldworth, gave the usual notice to the Fellows to assemble to elect a successor on the ensuing 13th of April. In the interim a Mandate was received from the King, dated April 5, requiring the Fellows to make choice of one Anthony Farmer, who was not a member of the College. Against this both the Bishop of Winchester, who was Visitor, and the Fellows, remonstrated, and besought the King to withdraw his recommendation, alleging that Farmer had not the qualifications required by the statutes, and was on many accounts an objectionable person ; and on the day of Election they refused to comply with the King's mandate, and placed Mr. John Hough in the Presidentship, who on the 16th was regularly admitted by the Visitor, before the Visitor had received an inhibitory Letter written on the 17th by Lord Sunderland. In obedience to the King's command a statement of the whole case was transmitted to Lord Sunderland by the Vice President and Fellows, when the King directed the Commissioners for Ecclesiastical Causes to proceed against them for this act of disobedience. They were summoned to appear in the Council Chamber at Whitehall on the 6th of June, to answer to such matters as should be objected against them. Of what passed on that day we have had an account in the Diary. The Vice President and a Deputation of the Fellows attended again on the 13th, and put in their answer, when the further consideration of the business was adjourned to the 22d of the month.

On the 22d they again attended, when, in justification of their conduct in refusing to elect Mr. Farmer, they delivered in a paper containing, amongst other objections to the person whom the King had recommended to them, charges of immorality, some of them of a very gross nature, but, gross as they were, supported by evidence delivered on oath. This is the paper of which the Bishop speaks in such strong terms. The issue was, as stated in the Diary, that the Commissioners declared the election of Mr. Hough void, and suspended Dr. Aldworth from his office of Vice President and Dr. Fairfax from his place as Fellow.

Thus stood the affair at the present time. Dr. Johnson, who dined with the Bishop after the sentence, is Dr. Nathaniel Johnston, from whose work, entitled, " The King's Visitatorial Power Asserted," 4to. 1688, and from the manuscript papers of Dr. Aldworth, now in the possession of Lord Braybrooke, this brief notice is compiled. In the latter we have a copy of the charges against Mr. Farmer, who, whether guilty to the full extent or not, was evidently an unfortunate choice on the part of the King in an affair in which great caution was peculiarly requisite, and the selection of such a person shews either inexcusable negligence in the King's advisers, or that they were driven to

23. I carried my son Gervas to my cousin Margaret's. Visited Mr. Gatford, Lord Privy Seal, Sir Edward Smith, Sir Roger L'Estrange, and dined at home with one of the Richmond proctors, and wrote to Dr. Hooke.

24. I sat for my picture at Mr. Kneller's; dined at home; treated with Thomas Fairfax about two York tenements; went with my wife to visit the Lady Warburton, Meares, and Dr. Constable, Mr. Rowland, Sir Roger L'Estrange, and Bishop Labourne.

25. I dined at Doctors Commons with the Bishop of St. David's at his consecration;[a] took up of Ald. Duncomb £26 19s. for interest, paid my first bond for Wigan £18 3s. due 1 Maii. Visited Lord Ancram, Sir Roger; fetched Charles from school; wrote to Bishop of Lichfield and Dean of Chester.

26. I assisted the Archbishop and Bishop of Rochester, at the consecration of the Bishop of St. David's at Lambeth, where Mr. Baker preached a good sermon. Dr. Johnson, Mr. Maidwell, and Mr. Rowland were his guests. I visited Bishop Labourne, Lady Warburton, and Mrs. De Puy. Sir Richard Wiseman and Mr. Fanshaw supped with us.

27. I sat for my picture to Mr. Kneller; answered Sir R. Wiseman's letter. Dr. Covel, Mr. Driffield, and Mr. Risdel, and sister Barnard dined with us. My son John signed an indenture and bond to Mr. Cradock not to meddle with the profits of the Commissary's place, during his life, and he was to send up the counterpart by Mr. Bowes, and the fees 40 guineas.

28. I went to Limehouse to see Gervas and Captain Hadock.

the greatest straights in finding persons who were willing to conform themselves to the King's inclinations. It may here be added, from Dr. Aldworth's Papers, that as early as possible after the receipt of the intelligence of the death of Dr. Clarke, namely, on April 1, the Bishop of Winchester wrote to the Fellows, urging them to proceed to the election with as little delay as possible, and recommending to them the Bishop of Man, Dr. Baptist Levinz, for their President. It would seem that he had a foresight of the King's design.

[a] Dr. Thomas Watson, successor to Dr. Lloyd. This was another unfortunate choice in this reign of a person to fill an exalted station in the church.

Sir Richard Wiseman, my father Wight, and brother Nelson dined with me. I gave Mr. Bowes a complaint of Dr. Samways against two incestuous marriages to deliver to Mr. Cradock. I sat to Mr. Kneller for my picture, and let Mr. Thomas Fairfax a lease of one house in York, for three lives, his own, his daughter Frances, and Elizabeth Brittain. The fine 20 guineas, the fees to Mr. Callis £2.

29. The Bishop of Lincoln came to visit me. I dined with Dr. Hawkins in the Tower. Went that night in the Bishop's coach to Windsor, his Archdeacon, and Secretary.

30. I carried the Bishop of Lincoln to the King's levee; after which he delivered his address, which was very graciously received. I brought him back to the camp, and dined with Mr. Ashton in Major-general Worden's tent; met my wife, son, and daughter, and returned after 8 at night from thence to Windsor.

July.

1. I was at Windsor at the King's levee, who went a hunting; visited the Dean of Winchester.

2. We continued at Windsor, dined with the Bishop of Oxon, and I supped with my Lord of Durham and Father Graham, at the Dean of Windsor's.[a]

3. I heard both sermons, and received the Sacrament with the Princess of Denmark in St. George's Chapel; and after dinner, with Sir H. Firebrasse, saw the Pope's Nuntio received in St. George's Hall, from whence I went to take leave of the Bishop of Oxon with Sir R. L'Estrange. I agreed with Sir Rob. Holmes.[b]

4. I was at the King's levee, dined with Major-general Worden in the camp, visited the Lord Dumbarton and the Earl of Peterborough and Mr. Sheffield, and so returned to London, where Sir Richard Wiseman and his friend supped with me.

5. I went with Sir Robert Holmes to my cousin Grahame to

---

[a] Gregory Hascard was at this time Dean of Windsor.

[b] Sir Robert Holmes was Governor of the Isle of Wight.

view his title to the fee-farm. Mr. Archdeacon Skelton[a] dined
with me. The Bishop of Lincoln visited me. I visited Col. Whitley
and Mr. Franklin. The Bishop of St. David's and Mr. William
Fanshaw supped with me. I wrote to the Dean, to my brother
Stow, Barnard, John Barnard, and Mr. Mason, for monies.

6. I went to meet the King at Whitehall; to visit the Bishop
of Lincoln; Sir Thomas Strickland, Sir Richard Wiseman, Sir
Thomas Meers, and Mr. Dean of Carlisle supped with me.

7. I visited my Lord Powis with Sir John Lowther; wrote to
the Bishop of Chichester, Dean of Ripon, and cousin P. Whalley,
and supped at Sir Edmund Wiseman's, with Sir Richard W. my
son, and Dr. Goodall.

8. I visited the Bishop of Lincoln and Sir Thomas Strickland.
Mr. Fanshaw and Mr. Dean of Carlisle dined with me; and the
Archdeacon brought the Bishop of Lichfield's address up, and I
went with my son and Sir R. W. to Windsor.

9. I was at the King's levee at Windsor, after which I delivered the Bishop of Lichfield's address by Archdeacon Vaughan,
and moved the King from Dr. Hooke about the dissenters refusing their offerings and small tithes under pretence of liberty of
conscience ;[b] who commanded me to write to him to sue them, for
that he never intended thereby to defraud the church of any of their
dues; and I dined with Sir Thomas Newcomb at Major-general
Worden's. The King got a fall that day in hunting, but, blessed
be God, no hurt.

10. I was at the King's levee, and took his commands to Chester, at which time I recommended Mr. Dean, Mr. Molineux, Mr.
Massey, my son John, and Mr. Fanshaw, to his favour, and having kissed his hand in the morning, I kissed the Queen's at night.

---

[a] John Shelton, Prebendary of Lincoln and Archdeacon of Bedford.

[b] Dr. Hooke, the Bishop's friend, had a very large and powerful body of Non-Conformists in his vicarage of Halifax. There were not fewer than seven congregations of
them when the Act of Toleration, two years after the time now spoken of, gave them
legal protection, beside the Quakers.

I was at both the sermons in St. George's chapel, and with the Princess at night, when the Nuntio paid his compliments to her.[a]

11. I came from Windsor with Sir James Boteler,[b] was entertained in the camp by Captain Lawson. Came home to dinner; went to Mr. Duroy's [?] to Fulham, who made me a present of his fine wares; took my leave of the Bishop of Lincoln, who promised my son a better, and Mr. Nicholas Poulton his prebend.

12. I dined at Lambeth, and took my leave, where his grace dispatched Mr. Dean of Chester's dispensation for Neston. Went to my cousin Graham, who dissuaded me from purchasing a fee-farm of Sir Rob. Holmes, as being revocable, because it belonged to the Prince of Wales.

13. I went to Jenkins with my wife, son, and daughter, to take my leave of Sir Thomas Fanshaw, and wrote to Mr. Sheffield about his money.

14. I dined with Sir James Boteler at St. Katharine's, with Dr. Hollingsworth and Dr. Hawkins, and took my leave of my old landlady in King Street.

15. My father, Mr. Nelson, Mr. Tayler, Mr. Chisnel et uxor, Dr. Johnson, Lady Wood and kinswoman, my cousin Margaret, Fr. Wingate, and Gervas, dined with me.

16. I dined with the Lord Yarmouth,[c] together with Sir John Pettus, Sir Edmund Wiseman, and took my leave of my cousins M. and W. at the Nag's Head.

17. Mr. Medwell's usher and Mr. Lowther dined with me; Mr. Wansford and Gervas, and Mr. Kidder, uxor et filia, and my sister Barnard.

---

[a] The Princess Anne, afterwards Queen, who has been named several times before. It would appear that measures were taken to interest her in the changes of religion which the King meditated.

[b] Sir James Boteler, made Master of St. Katharine's Hospital in 1684, from which office he was removed in 1698 by Lord Chancellor Somers.

[c] William Paston the second Earl, who had married one of the daughters of King Charles the Second.

18. I sat to Mr. Kneller for my picture. Received £20 3s. for tithe, till Lammas 1686, of Mr. Sheffield. Dined at home. Went with my wife to the goldsmith's. Bought two horses, one for eleven guineas, and the other £5 1s. Supped at home with Sir Edmund and Sir Richard Wiseman, Dr. Johnson, Dr. Evans, and William Fanshaw.

19. I paid my bills, took leave of Sir John Lowther and cousin Wiseman, and went that night out of town to the Saracen's Head at St. Alban's.

20. I went to my cousin Backwell's to Tyrringham to dinner, where we were kindly treated that and the next day, where my cousin Peter Whalley dined with us, and conducted us that night (July 21) to Coocknoe.

22. We lodged and dined at Coocknoe, where I paid my cousin £10 10s. [for things expended by him for A. C.] and £3 for charges at the christening of my cousin Ives his son Thomas Ives [to whom I was godfather]; and went that night to Northampton.

23. We came from Northampton to the Lord Sunderland's house at Althrop, thence to honest Mr. Hutchinson's to dinner, after to my aunt Haddon's, and thence to the Star at Coventry, where we supped and lay.

24. I dined with my Lord Bishop of Coventry; and supped with me my cousin West; and Mr. Wagstaff preached. The Bishop signed a dispensation to my cousin Haddon for non-residence upon Wolston, as my chaplain, and I the same to Mr. Griffith Vaughan, A.M. for non-residence on the rectory of Coppenhall in Cheshire, as his chaplain. I visited Mr. Hopkins and his lady, and received a letter from Sir John Bridgman to invite me to dine with him to-morrow at Castle Bromage.

25. I went from Coventry to Castle Bromage, where I was kindly entertained at dinner by Sir John Bridgman, and went from thence to the Four Crosses, a dear inn.

26. I went from the Four Crosses to Whitchurch to the George, where we had an excellent accommodation, and cheap.

27. I came into Chester by 10 in the morning, and went to evening prayer. Alderman Wilcox and Mr. Dean visited me and dined with me and two of Mr. Dean's nephews.

28. I gave Mr. Dean institution into the vicarage of Neston, and was visited by Mr. Massey before morning prayer, and again by him and Mr. Dean at supper, and by Sir John Arderne and his kinsman, and Mat. Anderton and Mr. Harpur.

29. I was at prayers. Mr. Brock the pewterer and Mr. Dean dined with me, and Mr. Dean took an information against Mr. Beckett, whom he committed the next day to the gaol. I wrote to Mr. Johnson the goldsmith and Sir Edmund Wiseman to pay him.

30. I accounted with Mr. Callis, received from him in full to this day £62 16s. Mr. Dean, Dr. Angel, and Mr. Mainwaring dined with me, Sir Thomas Grosvenor and his lady, the Governor, Col. Hastings, and another officer visited me. I paid Mr. Callis £11 for fees received at London, and Mr. Ward of Furnival's Inn is still in his debt for two York leases.

31. Mr. Wright preached well at the Cathedral. The Lady Grosvenor dined with us, and carried my daughter Sarah with her to a wedding in Wales. Mr. Thompson and his parishioners came to me about a burial place. Mr. Recorder and Mr. Dean were with me at night.

August.

1. I wrote to Mr. Ridley and to Mr. Bellingham, offering him his lease of Patrick Brompton for £74 fine. I received a letter from Major-general Worden, of his Majesty's resolution to come to Chester in his way to the Bath. I visited the Governor and the Recorder, and they me, with Mr. Massey.

2. I wrote to Mr. Dean of Durham, about the manner of the King's reception; to the Lord Peterborough and Major-general Worden, to invite the King to the palace; to Mr. Bellingham of his fine, to Edward Hodgson of his accounts, to Mr. Mickelton, of

his son's marriage, Mr. Cradock, and of Mr. Davison of Bam-
brough. I went out with my coach with the Recorder to meet
Baron Jenner, and supped with him at Mr. Alderman Simpson's.
Mr. Venables and Col. Whitley sent me each half a fat buck.

3. I dined with Baron Jenner at Alderman Simpson's, and
was very kindly entertained, with my son, and daughter, and wife.

4. We dined with Baron Jenner at Alderman Allen's.

5. Sir John Arderne and his lady, and son, Sir John Crew,
and 3 other ladies, and Mr. Booth, dined with us.

6. We dined at Sir Thomas Grosvenor's, and fetched my
daughter home. I tasted a hogshead of Obrian at Alderman
Mainwaring's, and received a letter from the Bishop of Lincoln,
of Winwick being void by the death of Dr. Scattergood,[a] and his
presenting my son John to it without fees, worth £160; and Mr.
Massey came to visit me.

7. I administered the Sacrament at the Abbey. Dr. Fogg
preached. Baron Jenner, Mr. Brown, and his other son and
friends, Alderman Simpson and his wife, and Alderman Allen et
uxor, Mr. Massey and Mr. Delavil, dined with me. Cos. Waite
and his wife supped with me.

8. I went from Chester to Wigan; dined with Mr. Shaw at
Warrington, carried Mr. Massey along with me, and supped at
Wigan.

9. The Lord Molineux[b] sent me a fat buck to Wigan; I
dined there with Mr. Mayor and the Recorder; went to the church
to prayers. After dinner called at Mr. Stanley's, and went to
the Anchor at Preston, where I met my Lord Brandon,[c] who
supped with us, and brought the Bayly of the town, and an im-
pertinent doctor of physic.

---

[a] Anthony Scattergood, D.D. Prebendary of Lichfield and Lincoln. He had been a
Fellow of Trinity College, Cambridge.

[b] Caryl Viscount Molineux.

[c] Viscount Brandon, eldest son of Charles Gerard, Earl of Macclesfield, a Colonel in
the army.

10. My Lord Brandon and my cousin Haddon came in the coach with us. We dined at Gasthang,[a] where the Bailiff of the town and the High Sheriff's brother met us. We called at the High Sheriff's house, from whence we went to Mr. Fenton's, the vicar of Lancaster, where my cousin Haddon and I lodged and supped, and sent our horses to Mr. Goodin's.

11. I carried my Lord Brandon and Mr. Massey with me in the coach two miles out of town, after I had been at prayers, and received a visit and present of three dozen of wine from the Mayor and Aldermen, and dined at the vicarage; with the High Sheriff to meet the Judges, after which I supped with the High Sheriff.

12. I went with Judge Powel to the Church; Sir Richard Allebone and the Catholics went at the same time to the school-house, where they had mass and a sermon; we had none of the best; 'twas preached by Mr. Turner, whom I chid for his extemporary prayer and sermon, of both of which he promised amendment for the future. I heard Sir Richard Allebone give the charge, in which he took notice, that no protestants but myself, my Lord Brandon, and Sir Daniel Fleming, came out to meet them, which was a great disrespect to the King's Commission.[b] I dined with the Sheriff, where I met my Lord Morley and Mounteagle,[c] and many of the Justices. I supped at the vicarage, with Sir Thomas Stringer, Serjeant Jefferson, Mr. Kirby, and Mr. Rawlinson, the patron of the living.

13. I wrote to Dr. Johnson, dined with the Judges, went after dinner to the Catholic Virgins, where Mr. Gooden lives with the Lady Allebone and her friends, and supped at the vicarage. Mr. Tildesley, whose grandfather Sir Thomas was killed by Wigan, sent me half a fat buck; Mr. Molineux, Mr. Braithwaite, Mr. Townley, Sir William Gerard, Mr. Poole, Mr. Labourne, &c. visited me.[d]

[a] Garstang.
[b] A curious fact, as indicative of the feeling of the country.
[c] Henry Parker, the last Baron of the name and family.
[d] These appear to have been all Roman Catholic Gentry of Lancashire.

14. I preached and confirmed 500 in the afternoon, most of them aged people, God be praised, at Lancaster. Was at the Mayor's banquet at the Judges' Chamber, saw and approved the address intended by the Grand Jury; took my leave of them, and was visited by most of the gentry at night.

15. I gave a license to Mr. Edward Nicholson to supply the chapel of Old Hutton in Westmorland, on Mr. Fenton's commendation of Lancaster; came out of Lancaster accompanied with the High Sheriff's brother, and many other gentlemen and clergymen ; staid within two miles to have the coach-wheel mended ; dined at Preston, where the Mayor and Aldermen, and Vicar, attended me with a banquet : came at night to Exton Varroe[?], six miles short of Wigan, with the Lord Brandon, Gerard,[a] and Mr. Massey, having met my cousin Waite at Preston.

16. We were met by Mr. Hadock and other neighbouring clergymen, and having breakfasted at Wigan, we drank with Mr. Shaw at Warrington, at Newton, and at Frodsham, and came safe to supper at Chester.

17. I wrote to Mr. Andrew Wilkinson[b] that he should have his lease for £114 18s. 8d. and not under. Mr. Barnard Howard, Lord Brandon, Mr. Norrice, and Mr. West dined with me. I visited the Governor and saw the Chapel. Lord Gerard, Colonel Hastings, Captain Dixy, and two other officers supped with me.

18. Lord Brandon and Captain   and Alderman Mainwaring dined with me. I granted a license to Hen. Newcomb de Tattenhall to be schoolmaster there, and several officers were with me at night.

19. Captain Povey and his lady, and Mr. Dean dined with me ; I visited Sir John Arderne and Colonel Barnard Howard ; Sir Rowland Stanley, Mr. Mainwaring, and Mr. Massey visited me.

20. Mr. Thomas Kent came to give me notice that he had re-

[a] Digby Lord Gerard of Bromley.
[b] Of Boroughbridge in Yorkshire.

signed Eccleston, and desired that I would not accept of it till he
had his year's tythe.   Mr. Trant brought me commendations from
the Lord Tyrconnell, and advice that he would set out on Monday
next for Chester, and desired my coach from Nesson.   Barnard
Howard and Mr. Dean dined with me and with the Recorder
supped with me.

21.   Dr. Folio's[a] eldest brother preached well at the Minster;
he and Mr. Trant dined with me.   The Governor and Major Barker, Sir Richard Maleverer, Mr. Fowles, Lord Brandon, and all
the officers visited me after prayers, and Barnard Howard and Mr.
Massey supped with me.   I received a letter from the Earl of Tyrconnel to provide him lodgings and his friends.

22.   I began my primary visitation of the Chapter of Chester,
and adjourned it to September the 6th.   I wrote to Mr. Ridley,
Sir Edmund Wiseman, Mr. Thomas Shepard, and Gervas about
Harry.   I went out to meet my Lord Tyrconnell with my coach,
and waited upon him at night at his lodging.   Barnard Howard
supped with me.

23.   The Lord Tyrconnell and all his friends drank their morning's draught with me.   Sir Rowland Stanley and Mr. Bapthorp
and Lord Brandon, and Barn. Howard, Sir Richard Maleverer,
and Mrs. Fowles, and two more dined with me, and four of them
supped with me; and I wrote by Mr. Withering to the Earl of Tyrconnell about the Recorder.

24.   The Lord Chief Baron and Attorney General of Ireland,
Sir James Poole, the Warden of Manchester, Col.   dined
with me; and the Lord Brandon, Col. Molineux, and three friends
of his, Captain Bellingham, Sir Richard Maleverer, and Capt.
Fowles supped with me and the Recorder, and Mr. Dean.

25.   Sir Richard Maleverer, Captain Bellingham, Mr. Fowles,
Sir Richard Nangle, Attorney General, Sir   Rice, Chief
Baron, Mr. Sabrando, dined and supped me.

---

* Foley.

26. The Lord Huntington and all his company dined with me; and many gentlemen supped with me.

27. Mr. Dean and Major Car, and seven or eight more, dined with me. His Majesty came to the palace in Chester about four in the afternoon.[a] I met him at the palace gates, attended by the Dean and Prebends, and about forty more of the Clergy, and afterwards introduced them to kiss his hand, Mr. Dean making an excellent speech to him. Then his Majesty went and viewed the choir; after that the castle, to which he walked on foot, and then returned to supper, and I waited at his cushion till I saw him in bed.

28. I was at his Majesty's levee; from whence, at nine o'clock, I attended him into the choir, where he healed 350 persons. After which he went to his devotions in the Shire Hall, and Mr. Penn held forth in the Tennis Court, and I preached in the Cathedral. His Majesty returned to dinner, on whom I attended, having introduced the Mayor and Recorder of Wigan, to whom he recommended their two former members, and also the Mayors of Preston and Lancaster; then I dined with my Lord President, and went to evening prayers, as his Majesty did again to the castle. After his Majesty was gone to bed, I supped with my Lord Feversham [b] in his chamber, having entertained Mr. Munstevens, Mr. Ware, and the Bishop of Man, in the study.

29. I was at the King's levee at six in the morning, brought my Lord Feversham, Lord Churchill,[c] and Lord Tyrconnell to drink coffee in the study; then attended his Majesty to his horse half an hour before seven, who went to heal and dine at Holywell,[d]

[a] The King left Windsor on the 16th: went in the first instance to Portsmouth, from thence to Bath, and then through Gloucester, Worcester, Ludlow, Shrewsbury, and Whitchurch, to Chester.

[b] Louis Duras, created Baron Duras by Charles the Second in 1672, succeeded in 1678 to the Earldom of Feversham, under a limitation in the patent to his wife's father.

[c] Afterwards the celebrated Duke of Marlborough.

[d] Saint Winifred's well in Flintshire.

from whence he returned at five at night [and took me into his closet for half an hour, where I gave him an account of what he had entrusted me with, which he graciously accepted, and assured me that I should hear from my Lord President before he called a parliament, and have sufficient instructions how to serve him. I recommended the Recorder Mr. Livesey to him, as a person fit to serve him in the next parliament; and Mr. Dean for better encouragement, because he was daily affronted for his zeal in his service by the Whigs, and told him of my Lord Cl.'s letter. I waited on him at supper, and after supped with my Lord Castlehaven, and Mr. Rider, and Mr. Griffiths. Mr. Williams and his son dined with me].

30. [I was at his Majesty's levee, and obtained a promise from him to make] Mr. John Warberton, M.A. of Brasen Nose, fellowship in All Souls'. After that he had mass in the presence chamber, where he eat. From thence I attended him into the choir, where he healed 450 people; from thence to the penthouse, where he breakfasted under a state, and from thence took horse about ten of the clock, from whence I returned to prayers, having taken leave of the Lord Tyrconnell. [The King told me that he had given a severe reprimand to the Governor for not promoting the address; and that he said it would not pass; to which the King replied, " Let me know what Alderman opposed, and I will turn him out;" whereas in truth he never shewed it them at all. The King commanded me to enquire out a chapel in the city, where it might be best spared, and give notice of it to my Lord Sunderland; to whom I lent my coach to go as far as Whitchurch.] William Pen gave me a visit, and promised to remember William Fanshaw. The King left £20 to the house servants.

Presents sent me when the King was at Chester: Sir Thomas Delves sent me a stag, which I gave, half to the King and half to the Lord President; Lord Brandon half a buck, Col. Howard half a buck, Lord Molineux one buck, Sir Thomas Stanley of Alderley half a buck; Sir John Crew six couple of rabbits and twelve pigeons; Mr. Tilsley a buck; and fruit from Col. Whitley's.

31. I wrote to Major-General Worden and to Sir Roger L'Estrange, and to Mr. John Warberton of Holcombe, about his ill-usage of H. Berry; and granted a collection to William Turner to the ministers of Lancashire, upon the recommendation of Lord Molineux and others. I sent for Captain Feilding, the Recorder, and others, to find out a convenient place, by his Majesty's command, in the castle or elsewhere, for the Roman Catholics' devotions.

September.

1. Being my birthday, I made my last will and testament. Mrs. Weston was with me after prayers; and I endeavoured to reconcile her to her daughter Peake and her husband, who, I find, hath carried himself as ill to his father-in-law as ever he did to his father in God. There dined with me Mr. Gooden the register and his wife, and friend Major Barker, and two friends of my Lord Chancellor's of Ireland, Mr. Foley, and Mr. Morris. After dinner Sir Thomas Delves, and Sir Thomas Mainwaring, and Mr. Booth, gave me a visit. Mr. Morris brought me a presentation to Bangor, concerning which I took time to deliberate. The Governor, Recorder, and Mr. Anderton, were with me at night.

2. Mr. Hunt dined with me: after Capt. Makartee, Mr. Gooden, a doctor of physic, and two more visited me.

3. Major Barker and another took leave of me for Ireland. I wrote to Mr. Mickelton and Mr. Wilson of my Durham accounts, and to Mr. Holmes. Mr. Crosland, and my Lord Marquess Powis master of the horse, were with me at night.

4. Mr. Murry preached a good sermon: Sir Thomas Grosvenor and my Lady, and Mr. Massey, the organist, and Mr. Ottway, dined with me after I had delivered the sacrament, and in the

evening the governor, Sir Thomas, and his Lady, and Mr. Massey, sat with us.

5. D. Angel, Mr. Hancock, and Mr. Warrey,[a] dined with me. Mr. Massey and Col. Shelden, and a captain, visited me after dinner. Mr. Leaston, at the general post office, sent me a news letter by Major-General Worden's order, for which I am to pay £2 per annum.

6. I adjourned the visitation of the Dean and Chapter till October 4th, by reason of Mr. Dean's sickness. Col. Shelden, and a Captain, and Mr. Massey, and a friend of the Governor's dined with me. Mr. Dalton and Sir Rowland Stanley visited me, and I visited Mr. Williams and the Recorder, where I met Mr. Venables.

7. The pewterer dined with us. I visited Mr. Booth where I met Sir Thomas Billet. The Recorder and Mr. Yates of Manchester supped with me.

8. Mr. Venables and his brother brought Mr. Biram of Prescot to me, who desired to have a curate in St. Helen's Chapel, into which the Presbyterians are now intruded, which I promised him, Mr. Dalton. I gave Mr. Anderton a visit at night, where I met Sir Peter Pindar and his son. My son Henry came down in the stage coach to Chester.

9. Mr. Andrew Wilkinson, of Boroughbridge, came to me to renew his lease of Kirkby Ravensworth. I went to Sir Thomas Grosvenor's to dinner, and Mr. Wilkinson and Mr. Morrice supped with me.

10. Mr. Brett from Mr. Pemberton, and Mr. Richardson, Mr. Wright's curate dined with me, and Mr. Morrice supped with me.

11. Mr. Thompson preached at the Minster. He, Col. Hastings, Capt. Herne, Mr. Wilkinson, Mr. Morrice, and Lieutenant   dined with me.

12. I went to Holywell with my wife, son, and daughter, Mr. Waite and his wife, Mr. Andrew Wilkinson, and Mr. Morrice,

---

[a] Qu. If for Morrey?

&c.; dined at the Star with them, and Mr. Roberts the priest, and returned at night to supper to Chester.

13. I sealed a lease of Kirkby Ravensworth to Mr. Andrew Wilkinson for his own [life] and Anne Jackson and Charles Wilkinson his brother, and the fine I took was £112. Mr. Morrice was with me about the patronage of Bangor. I dined with Mr. Mayor at his venison feast, and returned to prayers, and Mr. Wilkinson and Mr. Morrice and Tho. Waite supped with me.

14. Sir Rowland Stanley and Mr. Bridgman dined with me, and Mr. Packe, Sir James Poole, Lady Calverley, Mrs. Angel, and widow Whitley, visited me. Mr. Clegg brought Mr. Dean's letter, and the Subdean with him, to claim Lond Chapel, now possessed by Sir Thomas Clifton, and acknowledged by all to stand on his ground, but could make out no shadow of title to it, and so was dismissed by me.

15. Mr. Moseley of Amcotts, Dr. Fogg, Mat. Anderton, were with me. Mr. Massey dined with me, and I paid M. Anderton, by Mr. John Ashton's order, for 18 camp chairs. £5 1s.

16. We went after dinner to visit Mr. Chancellor and his lady, and Sir J. Arderne came to us at night.

17. After dinner Col. Whitley and his son, and Mr. Mainwaring, came to visit me, and I granted a seat in St. Margaret's Church to my Lady Calveley, who gave my son a Jacobus.

18. Mr. Archdeacon Allen preached at the Cathedral, after which in my private chapel I ordained

Deacon;—Roger Holt, ætat. 37, usher of the Free School, having testimonials from Humphrey Whittingham, Thomas Topping, and John Hancock, curate of Aldingham, in Lancashire.

Priest;—John Turner, ætat. 37, curate in the chapelry of Syddington, in the parish of Presbury, ordained Deacon by John, Bishop of Chester, Dec. 21, 1684. Testimonials from William Hayes, Thomas Whittingham, John Latham, and John Hancock.

My Lord Kilkerry and Col.   and the priests dined [with me]. Mr. Massey and Mr. Recorder supped with me. I visited Alderman Martin and Mr. Rainsford.

19. I went with Sir Thomas Grosvenor, Mr. Massey, and my son, to Liverpool; dined with my Lord Molineux at the Bowling green. Dr. Richmond and his son, and two more gentlemen, went to my Lord Molineux's at night, where I met Bishop Labourne, Mr. Townley and his brother, Mr. Goodwin, Mr. Labourne.

20. I continued with Bishop Labourne at my Lord Molineux's, and was treated very nobly. I wrote to the Marquess of Powis about Deputy Lieutenants.

21. I went at 11 of the clock from my Lord Molineux to Liverpool, where the mayor and aldermen met me in the church, and I commanded the churchwarden to set the communion table altar-wise against the wall. They gave me and Mr. Molineux and Mr. Massey a fish dinner, after which we were treated at Dr. Richmond's very kindly; then went on board the King's yacht; after which we were wet to the skin in going to Sir Rowland Stanley's, where we lodged, my lady then in labour.

22. Sir Rowland Stanley and Mr. Babthorp were very kind to us, and from them we returned to Chester before prayers. The Deputy Lieutenants whom I recommended to the Lord Powis the 20th instant, were, for the city, if he thought fit, because it was new and without precedent, the Governor, the Recorder, Aldermen Wilme and Willson; for the county, Lord Colchester, Lord Kilmurry, Sir Rowland Stanley, Sir James Poole, and Mr. Massey, the Governor, Sir Philip Egerton, Thomas Cholmondeley, Peter Legh of Lime, Justice Warren, Mr. George Oldfeild, Mr. Bruen of Stapleford, Sir John Crew, Sir William Meredith, Sir John Werden, Sir Jeffery Shakerley, Ralph Wilbraham, Thomas Needham, a Captain of Horse, and Mr. Molineux, or Sir Rowland Stanley, another;—Colonel Whitley, if they thought fit to make use of him. I forgot to mention Sir Thomas Stanley and the late High Sheriff of Cheshire, Mr. Davies, who are worthy men

and fit for it, Mr. Brown and Mr. Halton dined with me, two Oxford scholars. Mr. Morice, Mr. Shore, and Mr. Hilton came to me with a letter from the Master of the Rolls about Bangor and Worthenbury.

23. I wrote to Mr. Dean to invite him to meet Bishop Labourne at the palace; answered Sir John Trevor's letter about Bangor and Worthenbury.

24. I sent Sir Edmund Wiseman a bill of exchange from Mr. Hall of £50, and ordered him to receive 10 guineas of Mr. Cradock, and wrote to Mr. Mickelton and Sir John Trevor. I dined at Mr. Massey's, and brought Bishop Labourne and his brother George in my coach to Chester, who, with Mr. Mauson, Mr. Goodwin, Mr. Massey, and his sister, supped with us.

25. I ordained

Deacons.

1. Leigh, Peter, M.A. Wadh. Coll. letters; curate of Moberley. Age 23.

2. Heape, Richard, B.A. de Jesu Cant. Testim. Dr. Wroe, Mr. Gips, Crompton, Lomax; cur. de Charlton. Age 23.

3. Wilkinson, Chr. A. B. ædis Christi Cant. Coll. letters, Mr. Corles, Constantine, Hough, Heber, Tempest. Literæ dimissor. Ebor.; cur. de Marston. Age 24.

4. Lancaster, Isaac. Testim. Mr. Colby, Lupton, Lancaster, Barnet, Alcock; curat. de Lime Chap. Age 32.

5. Leech, Sam. A. M. de Edinb. Literæ de Col. Dr. Shippen, Dr. Wroe, Mr. Hyde, Lawton; cur. de Stockport. Age 27.

6. Whitehead, Tho. A. B. de Jesu Cant. Coll. Literæ, Dr.Wroe, Mr. Gips, Crompton, Lomax; cur. de Bradshaw cap. Age 23.

7. Battersby, John. Mr. Slack, Marsden, Ellershaw, Banks; cur. de Bolton. Age 23.

8. Sedgwick, Edw. A.B. de Jesu Cant. Literæ Coll. Mr. Lever, Smith, Haddon; cur. de Horridge cap. Age 23.

9. Gregson, William, B. A. Ænei Nasi. Literæ Coll. cur. de St. Michael's in Wire, Lancas. Age 23.

Priests.

1. Brett, John. Diac. per Episc. Lincoln. '78. A.M. Ænei Nasi. Literæ Coll. Dr. Fogg, Mr. Allen, Hancock; cur. de Tilston. Age 32.

2. Holt, Roger. Diac. per meipsum. Usher of the Free School. Presented to a sinecure. Aged 35.

3. Hollingworth, Benj. Diac. per Joh. Ebor. '85. A.B. Johannis Cant. Dr. Wroe, Mr. Gips, Crompton, Lomax, Harper; curat. de Ashton. Age 26.

4. Wells, Tho. Diac. per Tho. Lincoln. '86. A. M. Ænei Nasi. Literæ Coll. Curat. de Prescot. I gave him a license for to be curate of Prescot. Age 25.

5. Wood, Wm. Diac. per Tho. Carlil. '86. A.B. Trin. Cant. Literæ Coll. Mr. Hebden, Buck, Harrison, Wright, Slack. Literæ dimissor. Ebor. Curat. at Ilkley. Age 26.

6. Oddey, Tho. Diac. per Tho. Carlile, '86. A. B. Trin. Cant. Coll. literæ. Curat. at Coverham. Age 24.

7. Barnett, Dan. Diac. per Joh. Cestr. '84. Mr. Weston, Newcomb, Garreneiers. Curat. de Handley, to which he took a license. Age 28.

I confirmed in the private chapel Mr. Leigh, Mr. Leech, Mr. Wilkinson, and Mr. Sedgwick. Mr. Halton, M.A. of Brasennose, preached a good sermon.

All the clergy dined with me at one table, and Bishop Labourne, Sir Thomas Grosvenor and his lady, Mr. Massey and sister, Sir Rowland Stanley, and Mr. Babthorp, Mr. Mauson's brother and Mr. Peters.

28. I went with Bishop Labourne in my coach to Sir Thomas Grosvenor's, where we dined and supped and lodged.

27. Bishop Labourne went forwards for London, and we after dinner came to Chester, where my cousin West met us.

28. I was at the Minster prayers, where Mr. Chancellor invited us to dine with him to-morrow.

29. After sermon we dined at Mr. Chancellor's, and in the evening one of the King's messengers brought me a letter to attend his Majesty's service at London.

30. The King's messenger Mr. Leigh dined with me and Mr. Hugh Morris, whom I instituted to the rectory of Bangor. I answered the Lord Sunderland's letter.

October.

1. I wrote to Sir Edmund Wiseman, Mr. Ridley, and Dr. Johnston.

2. Mr. Foly preached well, and I administered the Sacrament. I gave a license to Thomas Baynham to be schoolmaster of Liverpool. He dined with me, and some of the officers. The Governor, Sir John Parker and his lady, and the Recorder, visited me.

3. I wrote to the Bishop of St. David's and Mr. Toures; visited Sir John Parker, and after sealed a lease of the rectory of Castleton in Derbyshire, to my son John Cartwright, for twenty-one years, of which seventeen are concurrent; and sealed Mr. Peter Yates his seat in Namptwich, which I had before decreed him.

4. I held my visitation; after which Col. Whitley, his two sons, and Alderman Mainwaring, dined with me, and Sir John Parker supped with me, having visited the Governor, Capt. Feilding, and Col. Hastings.

5. I wrote to Thomas Cradock about the Apparitor's place. Mrs. Ferimore was with me to demand payment of her husband's salary as Archdeacon, because she supplied the place till Michaelmas in preaching. I paid Joseph Lloyd his year's wages, for which he gave me his acquittance, £6. I bought the lease of

Wallezy of Mrs. Dorothy Brereton, and paid her £20 in hand, and gave her a bill upon Sir Edmund Wiseman for £80 more.

6. I sat in the Consistory, and examined Mrs. Weston's cause, and decreed she should pay but small costs. Mr. Subdean, Archdeacon Allen, Mr. Kent, Sir Thomas Grosvenor, Mr. Massey, Capt. Terne, Mr. Kent and others, dined with me. I sealed a lease of Wallezy to my son John Cartwright, for the lives of my wife Frances C. and Charles and Thomas; and ordered Sir Thomas Grosvenor to take livery and seizin. I concluded my visitation, and suspended Mr. Dean; the sentence to be published, if not taken off before, on Sunday three weeks.

7, 8, 9, 10, 11, 12. I came out from Chester in the stage coach for London, with four citizens, Mrs. Blagrave, Mr. Lloyd, Mr. Berry, and Mr. Kidley. We came on Friday night to Newport. On Saturday after dinner we called on Sir John Bridgman, and got to Coventry, where we were kindly entertained by Capt. Bellingham and his officers. We dined and supped with the Bishop on Sunday, and my son John preached in the afternoon. I visited Mr. Hopkins, and had his promise to do the King's business. On Monday we came to Northampton, where my cousin Whalleys, Mr. Archer, and all my kindred, supped with me at the Swan. The next day we came to Dunstable, where my cousin Backwell and his lady were; and on Wednesday we came safe, blessed be God, to London. I kissed the King's hand that night, and was graciously received by him.

13. I was at the King's levee, and after went with him into his closet, where he acquainted me that he, in confidence of my zeal to his service, had appointed me one of his High Commissioners for Ecclesiastical Affairs, and my Lord Chief Justice Wright and me to visit Magdalene College for their public and notorious disobedience to his commands, and commanded me to attend my Lord President for further instructions, which I accordingly did, and then went over to Lambeth to dinner, where I met the Earl of Clarendon and Bishop of Ely. From thence I went to Doctors'

Commons to Mr. Franklin and Sir Thomas Pinfold, with whom I advised concerning my son's usage by the Bishop of Peterborough, and wrote to the Bishop of Lincoln about it. From thence I returned to my Lord of Durham, and after to F. Petre's at Whitehall, with whom I discoursed the business of Magdalene College, and received papers from him.[a]

14. This being the King's birth day, I waited on him at his levee, to wish him many years, for which I daily pray, and received commands from Lord President to attend his Majesty at the Cabinet at six at night, which, having visited the Master of the Rolls, with Sir John Lowther, and dined with the Lady Peterborough, I accordingly did, where my Lord Chief Justice and I, in the presence of his Majesty and my Lord Chancellor and Lord President, received his commands to provide for our journey to Oxford on Tuesday next, and my coach not being in town, upon my Lord Peterborough's motion his Majesty promised me to give order to my Lord Dartmouth [b] to provide me one against the time, and

[a] The Magdalene College affair had proceeded in the following manner, since the time when the election of Mr. Hough was declared null, and the Vice-President, Dr. Aldworth, had been removed. When the orders of the Ecclesiastical Commissioners were sent to the Fellows, there was no one who would admit that he was the proper person to receive them, so that the messenger returned with them to town ; whereupon the Fellows were summoned to appear before the Commissioners for their contempt, and the messenger was directed to proceed again to Oxford and to affix the orders to the gates of the College. Meanwhile, a royal inhibition was issued against any proceeding to election to any office in the College by the Fellows. The Fellows appeared by a deputation, and alleged various irregularities in the form or delivery of the notice. On August 14 the King, abandoning Mr. Farmer, issued his mandate, addressed to Dr. Pudsey, the senior Fellow, and the rest of the Fellows, commanding them to admit to the office of President the Bishop of Oxford, Dr. Samuel Parker, to which they unanimously replied that they conceived the place to be already full. In this they persisted.
   The addition to the Commissioners of the Bishop of Chester, Sir Robert Wright, Chief Justice of the King's Bench, and Sir Thomas Jenner, one of the Barons of the Exchequer, was then made, and the Visitation of the College by the three new Commissioners resolved upon. This was communicated to the Bishop on the 13th, and he took his seat at the Board on the 17th.

[b] The first Lord Dartmouth, then Master of the Horse.

brought me to kiss the Queen's hand as he led her in to supper; and having received the congratulations of my friends [for having got the King's favour, after which all other things would be added to me.] I visited my Lord Peterborough in his bed, and returning to my lodging found Dr. Johnston, to whom [I gave the Answer to the Letter to a Dissenter, to carry to] Bishop Labourne, who came to London this night. [The King asked me concerning the letter written by Ld. Cl. to Sir J. A. blaming me and Mr. Dean for our zeal in the Address; and he promised to chide the Dean at his coming up, and desired me to refer the matter to F. P. who would cause him to make what submission I could expect.] I moved Sir Nicholas Butler for my cousin Fletcher, who promised to be kind to him for the future for my sake.

15. The Stewards for the Ministers' Sons waited on me in the morning, to request a Sermon of me at their feast, 1 Dec. which I told them I was willing to do, if I were master of mine own time, and knew I should be then in town, which as yet I did not. Mr. Timothy Evans, at Pickle Herring Stairs, who had been kind to my son Harry in bringing him out of the Indies, came to me. He has been commander of merchant-men to the Indies and Guinea, or mate, this ten years, and brought me four agates; who is desirous I would move Mr. Peepes to put him into his Majesty's service. His Majesty went a hunting, God send him safe home. Mr. Towres sent me a bottle of canary. Mr. William Fanshaw and Mr. Shores came to see me.

16. I was at the King's levee; after at Whitehall Chapel, where Dr. Goodman[a] preached. I dined with the Bishop of St. David's at Mr. Rowland's. I visited the Queen Dowager with Lord Preston, and returned to Whitehall, where I met Bishop Labourne, and kissed the Queen Consort's hand.

17. This is the first day of the 2nd year of my consecration, for which I bless God, and pray for his grace to enable me to serve him the better the longer I live. My Lord of Peterborough

---

a John Goodman, D.D. Rector of Much Hadham.

acquainted me, at the King's levee, that the King had given me £100 to fit myself for my journey to Oxon. I took my place in the High Commission, which was delivered to me by my Lord Chancellor, and the seal of the Court, in order to my Oxford journey. I dined with my Lord Peterborough and his lady, visited Sir Charles Scarborough, where I met Mr. Aires, the High Sheriff of Lincoln, and Dr. Johnson, with whom I went and hired a house in Lincoln Square, and stables, for £2 10s. per week, and supped at Mr. Toures', where I met Dr. Hedges and Mr. Atterbury. I visited in the morning Sir John Lowther, Lord Powis, and Lord Privy Seal.

18. This being St. Luke's day, on which I did my homage, I went to my Lord Chief Justice's chamber to meet with him and Baron Jenner, to adjust our business in order to our journey to Oxon. I dined with the chaplains, visited father P. and met the K. with him at Mr. Chiffin's at 4, and took his last instructions; went home, where I met Baron Jenner, Dr. Johnson, Dr. Evans, Mr. Elstob, and Mr. Poulton, and Sir John Lowther.

19. I breakfasted at Mr. Rowland's with the Bishop of St. David's, where Sir Richard Allebone was; and my Lord Chief Justice and Baron Jenner met me; from whence we took coach and called at Uxbridge, where we met Judge Powel and some other lawyers. We went to Wickham at night, where Capt. Lawson, C. Lloyd, and other officers there quartered, supped with us.

20. We came into Oxon, my Lord Peterborough's regiment receiving us at the town's end, where the Lieutenant-Col. and the rest of the officers dined with us. After dinner Dr. Halton, Dr. Hide, and Mr. Archdeacon Eaton, Dr. Adams, Mr. Brown, and Mr. Barnard, and Mr. Brooks and Mr. Wickens came to visit us.

21. We went to Magd. Coll. Chapel, where the crowd being great, and no preparations made for our sitting, we adjourned into the hall, where the crowd being great, we sent Mr. Atterbury for the proctors, who came accordingly to keep the peace. Mr. Tucker read the King's Commission. Mr. Atterbury returned the

citation on oath. Having called over the fellows, I made a speech for the occasion of the visitation,[a] and adjourned till 2 in the afternoon. We went to prayers in the chapel. There dined with us Mr. Barnard the proctor, Mr. Wickens, Mr. Brown, and the officers, and Archdeacon Eaton, who was rob'd the night before. In the afternoon we called over the college roll, and marked the absents. Dr. Fairfax, because in town, and not appearing, was pronounced contumacious, pæna reservata in prox. The buttery book brought up by the butler, and the statutes by Dr. Hough. Dr. Hough desired a copy of the commission in writing, which was denied him, and then he in his own name, and the greatest part of the fellows, said, He did submit to the visitation, as far as it is consistent with the laws of the land and the statutes of the college, and no farther; and said, he must suffer no alteration in any statute by the King, or any other; for which he had taken an oath, from which he could not swerve, and for which he quoted the statutes confirmed by Henry the Sixth, and their oath in them, that they should submit to no alteration made by any authority. Then Dr. Hough's former sentence of deprivation was commanded to be read; to which he replied, he was never cited nor heard, and therefore supposed the sentence to be invalid, and refused to submit to it, though he confessed he had notice of it. The college's petition to the King to recommend some other in Farmer's room, Number 4, was read; and asking them why they did not stay for an answer to it, Dr. Hough replied, their fifteen days were out before April 15, on which they had no other sent to them; and requiring him to give up the register, he promised we should have it tomorrow morning. Dr. Rogers' petition for the organist's place, worth £60 per annum, of which he says he was unduly deprived, was given in by Mr. Holloway and filed, and so we adjourned till

---

[a] This speech may be read at large in ' The King's Visitatorial Power Asserted,' p. 55-61. The further proceedings are related very fully in the Diary. Dr. Johnston's work has the date 1688 in the title-page. It appears by Anthony Wood's Diary that it came out in the month of June in that year.

the next day at 8. We visited Dr. Halton and the Bishop of Man. Mr. Spencer, Mr. Welsh, Mr. Holloway came to visit us.

22. We called in the steward with the books of leases and court rolls, which were delivered him back, till we made farther use of them. The butler brought the buttery book, and Dr. Hough being called in again, I told him, 'Doctor, here is a sentence under seal before us of the King's commissioners for visiting the universities, by which your election to the presidentship of Magd. Coll. is declared null and void, which you yesterday heard read, and of which you confessed yourself to have legal notice before it, being fixed upon your doors. This sentence, and the authority by which it was passed, you have contemned, and in contempt thereof have kept possession of the lodgings and office to this day, to the great contempt and dishonour of the King and his authority. Are you yet willing, upon second and better thoughts, 1st, to submit to this sentence passed by the Lords upon you, or not? 2ndly, Will you deliver up the keys and lodgings, as, by a clause in your oath at your admission, you are tied to do, for the use of the president, who has the King's letters mandatory to be admitted into that office?' To the first he says, that ' the decree of the commissioners is a perfect nullity from the beginning to the end, as to what relates to him, he never having been cited, nor having ever appeared before them either in his person or by his proxy; besides, his cause itself was never before them, their Lordships never inquiring or asking one question concerning the legality and statutableness of the election, for which reasons he is informed that the decree was of no validity against him, according to the methods of the civil law; but if it had, he is possessed of a freehold according to the laws of England and the statutes of the society, having been elected as unanimously and with as much formality as any of his predecessors, presidents of the college, and afterwards admitted by the Bishop of Winchester, their visitor, as the statutes of the college require; and therefore he could not submit to that sentence, because he thought he could not be deprived of his free-

hold, but by course of law in Westminster Hall, or by being some ways incapacitated, according to the founder's statutes, which were confirmed by King James I.' Then the Dr. asked, ' whether we acknowledged his title to the presidentship?' I replied, ' No; for we looked upon him as malæ fidei possessor, or an intruder.' He replied, that ' the Bishop of Winchester made him so, and said that he was satisfied in his own title, and therefore did not think himself concerned to apply to the commissioners till called, and that he expects legal courses should be taken against him, if he keep legal possession.' To which I replied, that ' the election was undue, because the King had laid his hands by his mandamus upon the college, which was an inhibition.' To the second question he answered, ' there neither is nor can be any president so long as he lives and obeys the laws of the land and the statutes of the place, and therefore he does not think it reasonable to give up his right, nor the keys and lodgings now demanded of him. He takes the Bishop of Winchester to be their ordinary visitor (and the King to be his extraordinary, as he believed, but it had been controverted whether the King had power to visit or not, in Coveney's case, 4 Eliz.) and yet he would deny him the keys, because he looks upon commanding the keys from him, to be requiring him to deliver up his office. He said he had appeared before us hitherto as judges, and that he now addressed to us as men of honour and judgment, and besought us to represent him as dutiful to his Majesty to the last degree, as he always would be, where his conscience permits, to the last moment of his life; and when he is dispossessed, he hopes we will intercede, that he may no longer lie under his Majesty's displeasure; or be frowned upon by his Prince, which would be the greatest affliction could befal him in this world.' Which having promised, I admonished him to depart peaceably from the president's lodgings, and to act no more as president or pretended president of the college, in contempt of the King, and his authority, 1mo, 2do, et tertio.

Mr. Leigh accused his contumacy, and prayed our judgment,

which was this : ' The Lords Commissioners for ecclesiastical causes and for visiting the university, have declared the president's place of this college to be null and void, and therefore we, by virtue of the King's authority to us committed, do order and command Dr. Hough forthwith to quit all pretensions to the said office, and that his name be struck out of the buttery book, and do admonish you the fellows and other members of this society no longer to own him as your president.'

Then we read the King's mandate for the Bishop of Oxon, and so adjourned to the same common room till 2 in the afternoon. Then Dr. Pudsey's letter, 28 Aug. '87, was read, which the doctor owned, and the fellows their consent to it. We asked them concerning the King's verbal command to them at Oxford, which they said was, to *elect* the Bishop, which they could not. We asked them why they did not *admit* him, which was all the King's letter required, to which his verbal command referred. Dr. Smith, Dr. Bayley, Dr. Hollis, Mr. Bagshaw, Hicks, Howner, Cradock, and Charnock, said they were not there. Dr. Stafford, Mr. Almond, Hammond, Rogers, Dobson, Bayley, Davies, Bateman, Hunt, Gilman, Pennison, Holden, and Wilks, said they were. Dr. Hough came in with a great crowd of followers, and said, 'Whereas your Lordships this morning have been pleased, pursuant to the former decree of the Lords Commissioners, to deprive me of the place of president of this college, and to strike my name out of the buttery book;—I do hereby protest against the said proceedings, and against all that you have done or hereafter shall do in prejudice of me and my right, as illegal, unjust and null; and I do hereby appeal to our Sovereign Lord the King in his courts of justice.' Upon which the rabble *hummed*, and Dr. Hough was accused by my Lord Chief Justice of bringing them in ; upon which he required the peace of him, to which he was bound in £1000 bond, and his two sureties in £500 each; and I gave the Dr. this answer :—' Doctor, we look upon your appeal, as to the matter and manner of it, to be unreasonable, not admissible, and

not to be admitted by us : 1. Because it is in a visitation, where
no appeal is allowable : 2ndly, because our visitation is by commission, under the broad seal of England, which is the supreme
authority, and therefore we overrule this your protestation and
appeal, and admonish you once for all to avoid the college and
obey the sentence.'[a] The doctor and fellows declared their grief
for the disorders of the crowd, and disclaimed having any hand in
it. Mr. Tucker read the paper, 4 Sept. attested by a public notary,
and delivered to the King; and the fellows acknowledged it to be
theirs, after which we adjourned till Tuesday at 8 in the morning.
The Vice-Chancellor,[b] Warden of New College,[c] and others, came
to visit us in the evening, and the Bishop of Man from the college, to beseech us not to animadvert upon the libel or the humming, but to accept their acknowledgments of the just respects
which they professed to owe us for our candour towards them;
after which we sent a messenger, with an account of what we had
done, to the King, and a letter to Lord Sunderland and Lord
Chancellor.

23. Having had prayers in our lodgings, we went to sermon to
Christ-Church, where Dr. Smith preached; from whence we returned to dinner, and with us the officers, Mr. Chetwin, Mr.
Brown, and our landlord and landlady. After which we went to
St. Mary's to church, where the preacher, Mr. Entwisle of Brasen-
nose, made reflections on some Bishops, of which the Papists had
hopes, but that they must destroy them all, before they could do
their business: after which we visited the master of Brasennose,
the proctor, the warden of All Souls,[d] and Mr. Clarke, where the
warden of New College came to us, and supped with the Bishop

---

[a] This speech is literally the same as that published in Dr. Johnston's work, which
was plainly, as to the portion of it relating to Magdalene College, prepared under the
Bishop's inspection, and with his assistance.

[b] Gilbert Ironside, Warden of Wadham College.

[c] Henry Beeston, D.D.

[d] Leopold William Finch, M.A.

of Man, where the provost of Queen's,[a] and warden of All Souls, and Mr. Chetwin, met us, and we staid till 8 at night. I received the Bishop of Oxford's letter and answered it.

24. I wrote to the Chancellor of Chester not to publish the suspension against the Dean till farther order from me, according to the Dean's desire, by letter. There dined with us Mr. Holloway, our landlady, two more; after which I went to Cuddesden to visit the Bishop of Oxon. Dr. Hough gave us a visit at my return, and then we went to the Vice-Chancellor's, from whence at our return we met with Mr. Charnock, and I received a nameless letter to caution us in the business of Magdalene College; and the Vice-Chancellor published a diploma against humming, &c. occasioned by Saturday's miscarriage in Magd. Coll. The Earl of Lichfield[b] sent us a brace of does. I went to Cuddesden.

25. We met at Magdalene, called over the fellows, &c. read the Bishop's proxy for instalment of Mr. Wickens, and then said; ' By virtue of the King's commission to us directed, we do order and decree the Right Reverend father in God, Samuel, Lord Bishop of Oxon, to be installed by his proxy Mr. Wickens in the president's stall in the chapel of this college forthwith, and the chapel doors to be opened for that purpose.' Which we saw effectually done by Mr. Leigh, who tendered him the oaths of president, allegiance, and supremacy; which having done, we returned into common room, where, having called in the fellows, &c. Dr. Stafford gave me a paper in the behalf of himself and the fellows, but subscribed by none but himself and Dr. Fairfax, of which having told him the danger, he humbly desired to withdraw it, to which we consented. We then propounded to them this question : ' Will you submit to the Bishop of Oxon, now installed your president by the King's mandate, *in licitis et honestis ?*' And they desired till the afternoon to consult together, and to give in their

---

[a] Timothy Halton, S.T.P.

[b] Edward Henry Lee, first Earl of Lichfield, Lord of the Bedchamber to King James, and Colonel of the Foot Guards.

answers in scriptis, which was granted them; and then we sent for a smith, and broke open the outward door of the president's lodgings, in the first room whereof we found all the keys, and left Mr. Wickens in quiet possession, and so adjourned. The Bishop's lady, Judge Holloway's daughter, and many of the officers dined with us.[a]

[a] Here the Diary ends, the volume being filled. It may be added, that of the Fellows two only, Charnock and Dr. Thomas Smith, submitted to receive the Bishop of Oxford as their President, and twenty-five were deprived of their Fellowships, and declared incapable of being admitted to any ecclesiastical dignity or benefice. At the Revolution, which quickly ensued, these illegal and arbitrary proceedings were annulled, and the Fellows restored ; as was also the President Dr. Hough, who lived to be a very aged man, and died Bishop of Worcester. On his monument in the cathedral is a bas-relief, in which he is represented in the act of protesting against the sentence of the Commissioners, and the words of his protest are engraved below.

THE END.

INDEX OF NAMES.

Cuddesden, Mr. 92 *bis.*

Dada, monsieur, 52, 53.
Dagget, Mr. William, A.B. 19 *bis.*
Dainton, (Daintree) 42 *n.*
Dalevil, captain, 36.
Dalton, Mr. 77 *bis.*
Danby Wisk, alias Danby super Wisk cum Yatherton, rectory of, 13 — 15 *n.*
Daniel, colonel, 35, 36 *bis.*
Darcy, colonel, 8. Mr. 12 *bis.*
Dartmouth, George baron, 84 *n.*
Davies, Alexander, esq. 24 *n.* Mr. 90. Mr. Henry, 79.
Davis, Mr. 5, 22, 31, 35 *bis*, 38.
Davison, Mr. 70.
Dawson, Gabriel, curate of Pilling chapel, 29. Sir William, 59, 61.
Daxon, Mr. 18.
Deane, in Cumberland, rectory of, 16.
Delamere, Henry baron, 21, 22, 23, 29 *note*, 49. *Vide* Warrington.
Delavil, Mr. 39, 70.
Delves, sir Thomas, 75, 76.
De Puy, Mr. 9, 59, 64.
Derby, William earl of, 18, 35 *ter*, *n.*
Divey, captain, 39.
Dixy, captain, 39, 72.
Dobson, Mr. 90.
Dodd, Mrs. 32, 33, 40.
Dolben, Dr. John, archbishop of York, 24, 45 *n*, 81. Mr. 52. Madam, 55.
Dolmon, Mr. 34.
Done, major, 28.
Douglas, Lord, 18. Colonel, 9.
Dove, Dr. Henry, 8, 45, 50.
Draper, Mr. 34.
Dreinards, Mr. 8.

Driffield, Mr. 64.
Drummond, Mr. 61.
Duck, alderman, afterwards sir John, 12, 12 *n*, 52.
Dumbarton, lord, 65.
Duncomb, alderman, 64. Mr. 8. Mr. William, 42.
Duppa, sir Thomas, 54.
Dupuy, Mr. 62.
Durham, 12.
Duroy (?) Mr. 67.

East, Mr. 55.
Eastham, parish of 23 *n.* 25.
Eaton, 38 *bis.* Mr. 32, 34. Mr. archdeacon, 86, 87.
Eccleston, 73.
Eden, sir Robert, 13.
Edwards, Mr. 37.
Egerton, Mr. 15, 28, 37. Philip, A.M. 18, 20. Sir Philip, 15, 18, 28, 35, 79. Lady, 28.
Eliot, Dr. 61.
Ellershaw, Mr. 80.
Elliot, Dr. 49, 50, 52, 54, 58, 59.
Ellis, Philip, bishop of Segni, 7 *note*, 51.
Elsley, Mr. 61.
Elstob, Mr. 44, 45, 49, 50, 53, 62, 86. Mrs. 48.
Errington, Mr. 56.
Essex, Mr. 20.
Etherick, W. 59.
Eubanke, F. 59.
Eubrack (?) colonel, 56.
Euxton chapel, 28.
Evans, Dr. 68, 86. Mr. Timothy, 85.
Ewart, Alexander, A.M. 33.
Exton, sir Thomas, 2 *note*, 49, 55.
Exton Varroe (?) 72.

ERRATA.

In p. 1, note ᵈ, *for* Dr. James Wood *read* Dr. Thomas Wood.
p. 66, note ᵃ, *for* Shelton *read* Skelton.

FINIS.